Both the for loop and while loop are loop structures to accomplish a repetitive job (i.e., <do something>). The for loop has provided an easy way to assign an initial counter value and to define how the counter value is incremented (or decremented) within the same line of code, while the while loop requires the user to define them in separate lines. The following two examples have an equivalent functionality.

```
for(int i = 0; i < 10; i++) {
        <do something>
}

int i = 0;
while(i < 10) {
        <do something>
        i++;
}
```

There is a good reason why we need the while loop option, in addition to the for loop. This example shows one of many circumstances when we prefer the while loop over the for loop.

```
boolean flag = true;
while(flag) {
        < commit planned operations, during which time
        the flag may be updated upon a certain codition
        change, e.g. the operation is completed, or
        failed for some reason.>
}
```

The do-while Loop

Java also provides a do-while loop structure:

```
do {
    <do something>
} while (expression);
```

The difference between do-while and while is that do-while evaluates its Boolean expression at the bottom of the loop instead of the top. Therefore, the statements within the do block (a.k.a. <do something>) are always executed at least once. You may try the following program to see a demo.

```
class DoWhileDemo {
    public static void main(String[] args){
        int count = 1;
        do {
            System.out.println("Count is: " + count);
            count++;
        } while (count < 1);
    }
}
```

Lab Work

1. Use the while loop to output "Hello!" 10 times.

2. Use the while loop to print out all integers from 1 to 25, inclusively.

Jumpstart Snowflake

A Step-by-Step Guide
to Modern Cloud Analytics

Dmitry Anoshin
Dmitry Shirokov
Donna Strok

apress®

Jumpstart Snowflake: A Step-by-Step Guide to Modern Cloud Analytics

Dmitry Anoshin
British Columbia, Canada

Dmitry Shirokov
Burnaby, BC, Canada

Donna Strok
Seattle, WA, USA

ISBN-13 (pbk): 978-1-4842-5327-4   ISBN-13 (electronic): 978-1-4842-5328-1
https://doi.org/10.1007/978-1-4842-5328-1

Managing Director, Apress Media LLC: Welmoed Spahr
Acquisitions Editor: Susan McDermott
Development Editor: Laura Berendson
Coordinating Editor: Jessica Vakili

Distributed to the book trade worldwide by Springer Science+Business Media New York, 233 Spring Street, 6th Floor, New York, NY 10013. Phone 1-800-SPRINGER, fax (201) 348-4505, e-mail orders-ny@springer-sbm.com, or visit www.springeronline.com. Apress Media, LLC is a California LLC and the sole member (owner) is Springer Science + Business Media Finance Inc (SSBM Finance Inc). SSBM Finance Inc is a **Delaware** corporation.

For information on translations, please e-mail rights@apress.com, or visit www.apress.com/rights-permissions.

Apress titles may be purchased in bulk for academic, corporate, or promotional use. eBook versions and licenses are also available for most titles. For more information, reference our Print and eBook Bulk Sales web page at www.apress.com/bulk-sales.

Any source code or other supplementary material referenced by the author in this book is available to readers on GitHub via the book's product page, located at www.apress.com/978-1-4842-5327-4. For more detailed information, please visit www.apress.com/source-code.

Printed on acid-free paper

To my wife Lana and my kids, Vasily, Anna, and Michael. Without your strong support and love, this book would not exist.

—Dmitry Anoshin

Table of Contents

About the Authors

Dmitry Anoshin is a data-centric technologist and recognized expert in building and implementing cloud analytics solutions. He has more than ten years of experience with data engineering and analytics and has worked across different industries in Europe and North America delivering end-to-end analytics solutions in a wide range of industries. His main interest now is cloud analytics with AWS, Azure, and GCP. He helps companies to modernize analytics solutions with cloud technologies and migrate legacy solutions to the cloud.

Moreover, he is the author of five books about various BI tools with PacktPub (*SAP Lumira Essentials, Learning Hunk (Splunk), Mastering BI with Microstrategy 10, Tableau Cookbook 2019, and Tableau Desktop Certitfication Guide*). He often presents at Tableau user groups, AWS and Azure user groups, and huge data conferences like Enterprise Data World and Data Summit. He leads the Tableau user group in Victoria, BC, and the Snowflake user groups in Vancouver and Toronto. In addition, he contributes to the leading Canadian analytics firm Rock Your Data (https://rockyourdata.cloud)and writes blog posts at https://medium.com/rock-your-data.

Finally, he mentors students in the data analytics program at the University of Victoria and shares cloud analytics knowledge, best practices, and real-world use cases.

Dmitrii Shirokov is a Data Architect & Cloud Analytics Consultant at Rock Your Data, focused on digital transformation, design analytics solutions, data integration and migration, data governance, and cloud/in-house infrastructure. With over 10 years of experience in data analytics and big data, he has the breadth and depth of experience needed to build mature analytical solutions. Before joining Rock Your Data in early 2018, he worked in different companies in tech consulting and banking sectors. Previously, he held various data-engineering positions focusing on data-driven business transformation.

Donna Strok loves all things data and for over 10 years has worked in the field with companies such as Expedia Group, JPMorgan Chase and most recently Amazon. She earned her Bachelors degree in Computer Science and her Masters in Computer Information Systems.

She resides in beautiful Seattle, WA with her cat Dwayne Johnson and in her free time enjoys the wanderlust of world travel. She's always on the on the hunt for exploring unique grocery stores and amazing hole-in the-wall restaurants, where some of her most memorable meals have been had.

Acknowledgments

I would like to thank the Apress team for the opportunity to deliver this book. Specifically, thank you to Susan McDermott, Laura Berendson, Rita Fernando, and Jessica Vakili for your support, editing, and guidance. We couldn't have done it without you.

A big thank-you to Kent Graziano who reviewed our book and added a lot of value to it as well as helped us edit and fine-tune the Snowflake information.

—Dmitry Anoshin, Dmitry Shirokov, and Donna Strok

CHAPTER 1

Getting Started with Cloud Analytics

"Don't shoot for the middle. Dare to think big. Disrupt. Revolutionize. Don't be afraid to form a sweeping dream that inspires, not only others, but yourself as well. Incremental innovation will not lead to real change—it only improves something slightly. Look for breakthrough innovations, change that will make a difference."

—Leonard Brody and David Raffa

Cloud technologies can change the way organizations do analytics. The cloud allows organizations to move fast and use best-of-breed technologies. Traditionally, data warehouse (DW) and business intelligence (BI) projects were considered a serious investment and took years to build. They required a solid team of BI, DW, and data integration (ETL) developers and architects. Moreover, they required big investments, IT support, and resources and hardware purchases. Even if you had the team, budget, and hardware in place, there was still a chance you would fail.

The cloud computing concept isn't new, but only recently has it started to be widely used for analytics use cases. The cloud creates access to near-infinite, low-cost storage; provides scalable computing; and gives you tools for building secure solutions. Finally, you pay only for what you use.

© Dmitry Anoshin, Dmitry Shirokov, Donna Strok 2020
D. Anoshin et al., *Jumpstart Snowflake*, https://doi.org/10.1007/978-1-4842-5328-1_1

In this chapter, we will cover the analytics market trends over the last decade and the DW evolution. In addition, we will cover key cloud concepts. Finally, you will meet the Snowflake DW and learn about its unique architecture.

Time to Innovate

As data professionals, we have worked on many data warehouse projects. We have designed and implemented numerous enterprise data warehouse solutions across various industries. Some projects we built from scratch, and others we fixed. Moreover, we have migrated systems from "legacy" to modern massive parallel processing (MPP) platforms and leveraged extract-load-transform (ELT) to let the MPP DW platform do the heavy lifting.

MPP is one of the core principles of analytics data warehousing, and it is still valid today. It is good to know about the alternative that existed before MPP was introduced, namely, symmetric multiprocessing. Figure 1-1 shows an easy example that help us understand the difference between SMP and MPP.

SMP - Symmetric Multiprocessing

MPP - Massively Parallel Processing

Figure 1-1. SMP vs. MPP

Let's look at a simple example. Imagine you have to do laundry. You have two options.

- Miss a party on Friday night but visit the laundromat where you can run all your laundry loads in parallel because everyone else is at the party. (This is MPP.)

- Visit the laundromat on Saturday and use just one washing machine. (This is SMP.)

It is obvious that running six washing machines at the same time is faster than running one at a time. It is this linear scalability of MPP systems that allows us to accomplish our task faster. Table 1-1 compares the SMP and MPP systems. If you work with a DW, you are probably aware of these concepts. Snowflake innovates in this area and actually combines SMP and MPP.

Table 1-1. *MPP vs. SMP*

Model	Description
Massively parallel processing (MPP)	The coordinated processing of a single task by multiple processors, with each processor using its own OS and memory and communicating with each other using some form of messaging interface. Usually MPP is a share-nothing architecture.
Symmetric multiprocessing (SMP)	A tightly coupled multiprocessor system where processors share resources such as single instances of the operating system (OS), memory, I/O devices, and a common bus. SMP is a shared-disk architecture.

In our past work, Oracle was popular across enterprise organizations. All the DW solutions had one thing in common: they were extremely expensive and required the purchase of hardware. For consulting companies, the hardware drove revenue; you could have an unprofitable consulting project, but a hardware deal would cover the yearly bonus.

Later, we saw the rise of Hadoop and big data. The Internet was full of news about the replacement of traditional DWs with Hadoop ecosystems. It was a good time for Java developers, who could enjoy coding and writing Map Reduce jobs until the community released a bunch of SQL tools such as Hive, Presto, and so on. Instead of learning Java, personally we applied Pareto principles, where we could solve 20 percent of tasks using traditional DW platforms and SQL to bring 80 percent of the value. (In reality, we think it was more like 80 percent of the cases produced 95 percent of the value.)

Later, we saw the rise of data science and machine learning, and developers started to learn R and Python. But we found we still should have ELT/ETL and DW in place; otherwise, these local R/Python scripts didn't have any value. It was relatively easy to get a sample data set and build a model using data mining techniques. However, it was a challenge to automate and scale this process because of a lack of computing power.

Then came data lakes. It was clear that a DW couldn't fit all the data, and we couldn't store all the data in a DW because it was expensive. If you aren't familiar with data lakes, see `https://medium.com/rock-your-data/ getting-started-with-data-lake-4bb13643f9`.

Again, some parties argued that data lakes were new DWs, and everyone should immediately migrate their traditional solutions to data lakes using the Hadoop technology stack. We personally didn't believe that data lakes could replace the traditional SQL DWs based on our experience with BI and business users. However, a data lake could complement an existing DW solution when there was a big volume of unstructured data and we didn't want to leverage the existing DW because it lacked computing power and storage capabilities. Apache products such as Hive, Presto, and Impala helped us to get SQL access for big data storage and leverage data lake data with traditional BI solutions. It is obvious that this path was expensive but could work for big companies with resources and strong IT teams.

In 2013, we heard about DWs in the cloud, namely, Amazon Redshift. We didn't see a difference between the cloud edition of Amazon Redshift and the on-premise Teradata, but it was obvious that we could get the same results without buying an extremely expensive appliance. Even at that time, we noticed the one benefit of Redshift. It was built on top of the existing open source database Postgres. This meant we didn't really need to learn something new. We knew the MPP concept from Teradata and we knew Postgres, so we could start to use Redshift immediately. It was definitely a breath of fresh air in a world of big dinosaurs like Oracle and Teradata.

It should be obvious to you that Amazon Redshift wasn't a disruptive innovation. It was an incremental innovation that built on a foundation already in place. In other words, it was an improvement to the existing technology or system. That is the core difference between Snowflake and other cloud DW platforms.

Amazon Redshift became quite popular, and other companies introduced their cloud DW platforms. Nowadays, all big market vendors are building a DW solution for the cloud.

As a result, Snowflake was the disruptive innovation. The founders of Snowflake collected all the pain points of the existing DW platforms and came up with a new architecture and new product that addresses modern data needs and allows organization to move fast with limited budgets and small teams. If you are interested in a market overview of DW solutions, refer to Gartner's Quadrant for Data Management Solutions for Analytics, as shown in Figure 1-2.

Figure 1-2. *Gartner's Quadrant for Data Management Solutions for Analytics. Source: Smoot, Rob; "Snowflake Recognized as a Leader by Gartner: Third Consecutive Year Positioned in the Magic Quadrant Report," Jan 23, 2019,* https://www.snowflake.com/ blog/snowflake-recognized-as-a-leader-by-gartner-third-consecutive-year-positioned-in-the-magic-quadrant-report/

Everyone has their own journey. Some worked with big data technologies like Hadoop; others spent time with traditional DW and BI solutions. But all of us have a common goal of helping our organizations to be truly data-driven. With the rise of cloud computing, we have many new opportunities to do our jobs better and faster. Moreover, cloud computing opened new ways of doing analytics. Snowflake was founded in 2012, came out in stealth mode in October 2014, and became generally available in June 2015. Snowflake brought innovation into the data warehouse world, and it is the new era of data warehousing.

Key Cloud Computing Concepts

Before jumping into Snowflake, we'll cover key cloud fundamentals to help you better understand the value of the cloud platform.

Basically, cloud computing is a remote virtual pool of on-demand shared resources offering compute, storage, database, and network services that can be rapidly deployed at scale. Figure 1-3 shows the key elements of cloud computing.

Compute   Databases   Storage   Network   ML/AI

Figure 1-3. *Key terms of cloud computing*

Table 1-2 defines the key terms of cloud computing. These are the building blocks for a cloud analytics solution as well as the Snowflake DW.

Table 1-2. *Key Terms for Cloud Computing*

Term	Description
Compute	The "brain" to process our workload. It has the CPUs and RAM to run workloads and processes, in our case, data.
Databases	Traditional SQL or NoSQL databases that we can leverage for our applications and analytics solutions in order to store structure data.
Storage	Allows us to save and store data in raw format as files. It could be traditional text files, images, or audio. Any resource in the cloud that can store data is a storage resource.
Network	Provides resources for connectivity between other cloud services and consumers.
ML/AI	Provides special types of resources for heavy computations and analytics workloads.

It is important to mention hypervisors as a core element of cloud computing. Figure 1-4 shows a host with multiple virtual machines and a hypervisor that is used to create a virtualized environment that allows multiple VMs to be deployed on a single physical host.

Hypervisor - software used to create the virtualized environment allowing for multiple VMs to be installed on the same host

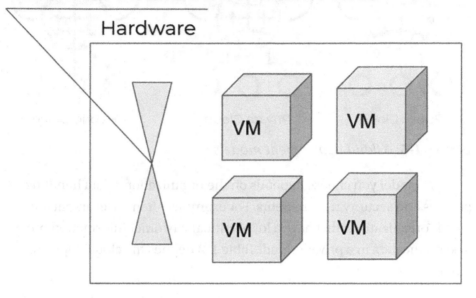

Figure 1-4. *Role of hypervisor*

Virtualization gives us the following benefits:

- Reduces capital expenditure

- Reduces operating costs

- Provides a smaller footprint

- Provides optimization for resources

There are three cloud deployment models, as shown in Figure 1-5.

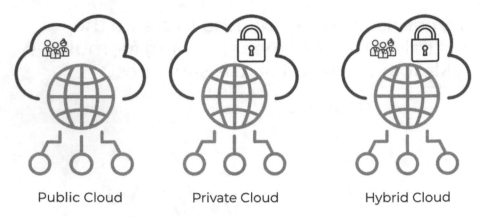

Public Cloud   Private Cloud   Hybrid Cloud

Figure 1-5. *Cloud deployment models*

The model you choose depends on the organization's data handling policies and security requirements. For example, often government and health organizations that have a lot of critical customer information prefer to keep the data in a private cloud. Table 1-3 defines the cloud deployment models.

Table 1-3. *Cloud Deployment Models*

Model	Description
Public cloud	The service provider opens up the cloud infrastructure for organizations to use, and the infrastructure is on the premises of the service provider (data centers), but it is operated by the organization paying for it.
Private cloud	The cloud is solely owned by a particular institution, organization, or enterprise.
Hybrid cloud	This is a mix of public and private clouds.

In most cases, we prefer to go with a public cloud. AWS, Azure, and GCP all are public clouds, and you can start building solutions and applications immediately.

It is also good to know about cloud service models (as opposed to on-premise solutions). Figure 1-6 shows three main service models with an easy analogy "Hamburger as a Service".

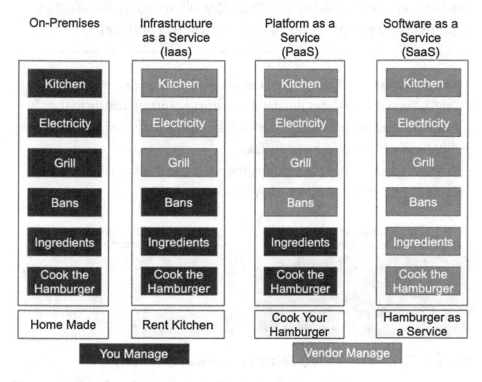

Figure 1-6. *Cloud service models, pizza as a service*

One example of IaaS is a cloud virtual machine. Amazon EC2 is an example of IaaS. Amazon Elastic MapReduce (i.e., managed Hadoop) is an example of PaaS, and DynamoDB (AWS NoSQL database) is an example of SaaS that is completely managed for you.

Note   In a cloud software distribution model, SaaS is the most comprehensive service, and it abstracts much of the underlying hardware and software maintenance from the end user. It is characterized by a seamless, web-based experience, with as little management and optimization as possible required of the end user. The IaaS and PaaS models, comparatively, often require significantly more management of the underlying hardware or software.

Snowflake is a SaaS model also known as *data warehouse as a service* (DWaaS). Everything—from the database storage infrastructure to the compute resources used for analysis and the optimization of data within the database—is handled by Snowflake.

A final aspect of cloud computing theory is the shared responsibility model (SRM). Figure 1-7 shows a key elements of SRM.

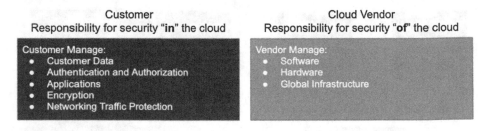

Figure 1-7. *Cloud Vendors Shared Responsibility Model*

SRM has many attributes, but the main idea is that the cloud vendor is responsible for the security *of* the cloud, and the customers are responsible for the security *in* the cloud. This means that the clients should define their security strategies and leverage best practices for their data in order to keep it secure.

When we talk about the cloud, you should know that cloud resources are hosted in data centers and there is a concept of a region. You can find information about Snowflake availability for the different cloud vendors and regions at https://docs.snowflake.net/manuals/user-guide/intro-regions.html.

Before moving to the next section, refer to Figure 1-8, which shows how long data takes to upload to the cloud; this reference comes from Google Cloud Platform presentation.

Bandwidth	Data Size								
	1 GB	10 GB	100 GB	1 TB	10 TB	100 TB	1 PB	10 PB	100 PB
1 Mbps	3 hours	30 hours	12 days	124 days	3 years	34 years	340 years	3404 years	34048 years
10 Mbps	18 minutes	3 hours	30 hours	12 days	124 days	3 years	34 years	340 years	3404 years
100 Mbps	2 minutes	18 minutes	3 hours	30 hours	12 days	124 days	3 years	34 years	340 years
1 Gbps	11 seconds	2 minutes	18 minutes	3 hours	30 hours	12 days	124 days	3 years	34 years
10 Gbps	1 second	11 seconds	2 minutes	18 minutes	3 hours	30 hours	12 days	124 days	3 years
100 Gbps	0.1 seconds	1 second	11 seconds	2 minutes	18 minutes	3 hours	30 hours	12 days	124 days

Figure 1-8. *Modern bandwidth*

This table is a useful reference when migrating a DW from an on-premise solution to the cloud. You will learn more about DW migration and modernization in Chapter 14.

Meet Snowflake

Snowflake is the first data warehouse that was built for the cloud from the ground up, and it is a first-in-class data warehouse as a service. Snowflake runs on the most popular cloud providers such as Amazon Web Services and Microsoft Azure. Moreover, Snowflake has announced availability on Google Cloud Platform. As a result, we can deploy the DW platform on any of the major cloud vendors. Snowflake is faster and easier to use and far more flexible than a traditional DW. It handles all aspects of authentication, configurations, resource management, data protection, availability, and optimization.

It is easy to get started with Snowflake. You just need to choose the right edition of Snowflake and sign up. You can start with a free trial and learn about the key features of Snowflake or compare it with other DW platforms at `https://trial.snowflake.com`. You can immediately load your data and get insights. All the components of Snowflake services run in a public cloud infrastructure.

Note   Snowflake cannot be run on private cloud infrastructures (on-premises or hosted). It is not a packaged software offering that can be installed by a user. Snowflake manages all aspects of software installation and updates.

Snowflake was built from the ground up and designed to handle modern big data and analytics challenges. It combines the benefits of both SMP and MPP architectures and takes full advantage of the cloud. Figure 1-9 shows the architecture of Snowflake.

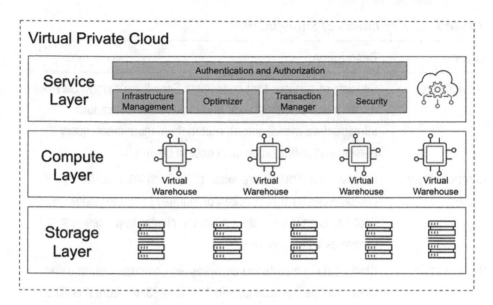

Figure 1-9. *Snowflake architecture*

Similar to an SMP architecture, Snowflake uses a central storage that is accessible from all the compute nodes. In addition, similar to an MPP architecture, Snowflake processes queries using MPP compute clusters, also known as *virtual warehouses*. As a result, Snowflake combines the simplicity of data management and scalability with a shared-nothing architecture (like in MPP).

As shown in Figure 1-9, the Snowflake architecture consists of three main layers. Table 1-4 describes each layer.

Table 1-4. *Key Layers of Snowflake*

Layer	Description
Service layer	Consists of services that coordinate Snowflake's work. Services run on a dedicated instance and include authentication, infrastructure management, metadata management, query parsing and optimization, and access control.
Compute layer	Consists of a virtual warehouse (VW). Each VW is an MPP compute cluster that consists of multiple compute nodes. Each VM is an independent compute cluster that doesn't share resources with other VMs.
Storage layer	Stores data in an internal compressed columnar format using cloud storage. For example, in AWS it is S3; in Azure it is Blob storage. Snowflake manages all aspects of data storage, and customers don't have direct access to file storage. Data is accessible only via SQL.

In other words, Snowflake offers almost unlimited computing and storage capabilities by utilizing cloud storage and computing. Let's look at a simple example of a traditional organization with a DW platform. For example, say you have a DW, and you run ETL processing overnight. During heavy ETL processing, business users can't use the DW a lot, and there aren't many resources available. At the same time, the marketing department should run complex queries for calculating the attribution model. The inventory team should run their reports and optimize inventory. In other words, every process and every team in the organization is important, but the DW is a bottleneck. In the case of Snowflake, every team or department can have its own virtual warehouse that can be scaled up and down immediately depending on the requirements. Moreover, the ETL process can have its own virtual warehouse that is running only overnight. This means the DW isn't a bottleneck anymore and allows the organization to unlock its data's potential. Moreover, the organization will pay only for the resources it uses. You don't have to buy expensive appliances or think about future workloads. Snowflake is truly democratizing data and gives almost unlimited power to business users.

In addition to scalability and simplicity, Snowflake offers many more unique features that didn't exist before and aren't available in other DW platforms (cloud or on-premise) such as data sharing, time travel, database replication and failover, zero-copy cloning, and more that you will learn in this book.

Summary

In this chapter, we briefly reviewed the history of data warehousing and covered the fundamentals of cloud computing. This information gave you some background so that you have a better understanding of why Snowflake was brought to the market and why the cloud is the future of data warehousing and modern analytics. Finally, you learned about the unique architecture of Snowflake and its key layers. In the next chapter, you will learn how to start working with Snowflake.

## CHAPTER 2

Getting Started with Snowflake

Congratulations on choosing to get started with Snowflake! In this chapter, we will cover the following topics:

- Planning

- Creating your Snowflake account

- Connecting to Snowflake

By the end of this chapter, you will be ready to begin your cloud analytics journey and follow along with the remaining chapters of this book. In the "Planning" section, we will cover what decisions should be made before creating your Snowflake account. These considerations include pricing and region choices. We will also briefly introduce the Snowflake web interface.

Planning

You need to consider the following before creating your Snowflake account:

- Snowflake editions

- Cloud providers and regions

- Snowflake pricing model

- Types of Snowflake tools

© Dmitry Anoshin, Dmitry Shirokov, Donna Strok 2020
D. Anoshin et al., *Jumpstart Snowflake*, https://doi.org/10.1007/978-1-4842-5328-1_2

Deciding on a Snowflake Edition

When you create your Snowflake account, you will be asked to choose a Snowflake edition. Snowflake offers five account types, and each one provides progressively more features.

Table 2-1 gives a high-level overview of the Snowflake editions and what features are considered the selling points. Please refer to Snowflake's online pricing for the latest edition offerings and features (`https://www.snowflake.com/pricing`).

Table 2-1. *Snowflake Editions*

Standard	Premier	Enterprise	Business Critical	Virtual Private Snowflake
Dedicated virtual warehouse	All Standard edition features	All Premier edition features	All Enterprise edition features	All Enterprise Sensitive edition features
Cross regional and cloud platform data sharing	Premier Support 24 / 7 including fast response time	Multi-cluster warehouse	HIPAA support	Virtual servers with encryption key in memory
Database replication	Refunds for outages	Ninety days of time travel	PCI compliant	Dedicated metadata store
Full Support only during business hours		Materialized views	All data are encrypted	Extra operational dashboards
Encryption in transit and at rest		Encrypted data is auto-rekeyed annually	Enhanced security policy	
One day of time travel		AWS PrivateLink support available for an additional fee	Tri-secret secure with customer managed keys	
Federated authentication			Database failover to ensure business continuity	
			AWS PrivateLink support	

Choosing a Cloud Provider and Region

At the time of this publication, a Snowflake account can be hosted on either Amazon Web Services (AWS) or Microsoft Azure. Each cloud provider has data centers in many locations around the world. These locations are referred to as *regions*. Transferring data between regions can have cost implications. Therefore, region considerations are important because the costs can vary depending on your requirements.

Multiple regions might be necessary to address global data access speeds as well as replication needs. For example, if you have users located in different parts of the world, it might make sense to replicate or partition the data closer to your users. If you have a use case for multiple regions, then you will need to create a Snowflake account for each region. We will talk about solving multiple-region issues in later chapters.

Note   Snowflake accounts do not support more than one region. You will need to create a Snowflake account for each region.

Regions dictate only the geographic location of where the data is stored and the compute resources are provisioned, not the usage of the data. The usage of the data may occur from anywhere in the world. Also, the cloud platform that is chosen for each Snowflake account is completely independent from your other Snowflake accounts. You may choose to use a mix of cloud providers and regions; however, be aware that this will impact the cost of transferring data into your Snowflake account. Also, there are some limitations with using Azure as a cloud provider, as described in Table 2-2.

Table 2-2. *Limitations to Your Snowflake Account When Hosted on Microsoft Azure*

Snowflake editions impacted	Virtual Private Snowflake (VPS) is not currently available on Azure but is planned to be released shortly. Check with the Snowflake web site for more details: `https://docs.snowflake.net/manuals/user-guide/intro-editions.html`
Security and data encryption	No support for encryption with customer-managed keys.
	No support for secure connectivity to customer-owned virtual networks.
Data loading	To access S3 from Azure, IAM policies must allow for Snowflake access.
Third-party application support	Check with your third-party partner to determine whether Azure is supported.
	These partners do support Azure: Alooma, Attunity, Databricks, Fivetran, Informatica, Looker, Matillion, MicroStrategy, Periscope, Power BI, Qubole, Sigma Computing, Stitch, Tableau, Talend, and Wherescape.

Examining Snowflake's Pricing Model

The pricing model is an attractive feature of Snowflake. This is because Snowflake charges only for what is used. The storage and compute resource costs are based on the amount of compressed data stored in the database tables and whatever is needed for data recovery. The virtual warehouse size determines the number of servers per cluster and what the compute costs will be. The pricing model uses *credits*, and credits are billed by full hour. Virtual warehouse sizes come in eight T-shirt sizes, as noted in Table 2-3.

Table 2-3. *Credits Charged by Full Hour Based on Virtual Warehouse Size*

X-Small	Small	Medium	Large	X-Large	2X-Large	3X-Large	4X-Large
1	2	4	8	16	32	64	128

Note   Credits are billed on a per-second basis only when virtual warehouses are running. If a virtual warehouse is suspended, it will not accrue charges.

If a virtual warehouse needs to be resized, credits are billed only for the additional increase or decrease in servers. For example, if your virtual warehouse is increasing from Large to X-Large, you will be charged per minute for each cluster being added. In this case, eight additional credits are accrued for that minute during the increase. Also, each time a server is started or stopped, there is a one-minute minimum billing charge even if it took less time. After the minute of billing has occurred, then charges go back to per-second billing. Refer to the Snowflake web site to get the current pricing per credits in your currency.

Other Pricing Considerations

You can choose to leave your data in the Snowflake database. But if you need to transfer or copy your data out of Snowflake and into another external storage location (i.e., AWS S3), Snowflake will charge for the query compute costs associated with the export. Also, if you're going to export your data out of Snowflake and into a cloud storage such as S3 or Azure Blob, there are additional egress charges for that if the location is either in a different region or with a different cloud storage provider.

Remember   Snowflake does not charge to load data into your Snowflake environment from any external stage; however, your cloud storage provider (Amazon S3 or Microsoft Azure) might charge a separate *egress* fee if your data storage is located in a region or network different from your Snowflake account.

Examining Types of Snowflake Tools

Snowflake can be accessed in several ways: through a UI, command line, JDBC/ODBC driver, or many third-party partner tools.

- Snowflake web interface. Most browsers can support the Snowflake web interface. For minimum versions, check the Snowflake web site. Snowflake recommends Google Chrome (minimum version).

- SnowSQL, the Snowflake command-line client.

- Any client application connected via JDBC or ODBC.

- Third-party partners that have been built with Snowflake capabilities, like Tableau and Matillion.

Snowflake Web Interface

You can use any of the browser versions in Table 2-4 to access the Snowflake web interface. Snowflake recommends using Google Chrome because the other browsers have not been tested as much as Chrome has. If any issues occur with the browser in the versions listed in Table 2-4, contact Snowflake Support for help. We will go through the Snowflake web interface more extensively later in this chapter.

Table 2-4. *Browsers Supported by the Snowflake Web Interface*

Browsers	Versions
Chrome	47+
Safari	9+
Firefox	45+
Internet Explorer	11+
Opera	36+
Edge	12+

SnowSQL

SnowSQL is a command-line client for connecting to and using Snowflake. SnowSQL can be installed on any Red Hat–compatible Linux operating system, macOS (64-bit), and Windows (64-bit). Other operating systems have not been tested and may not work with SnowSQL. There are some Linux systems that may not have all the needed libraries used by the SnowSQL client. SnowSQL is available for download from the Snowflake web interface as well as the Snowflake web site. We will cover SnowSQL in later chapters of this book.

JDBC and ODBC OS Platform Requirements

Both the Snowflake JDBC (64-bit) and ODBC (32-bit and 64-bit) drivers can be installed on Linux, macOS, and Windows. The JDBC driver is available for download from the Maven Central Repository at http://search.maven.org/. The ODBC driver is available on the Snowflake Client Driver Repository at https://sfc-repo.snowflakecomputing.com/odbc/index.html. The ODBC driver can also be downloaded from the Snowflake console. Windows users may need to install .NET drivers prior to the installation of the ODBC driver.

Third-Party Partners

In later chapters we will go over how the third-party partners Matillion and
Tableau use Snowflake. Right now, Snowflake makes it easy to integrate
with some of the more popular third-party tools like Databricks, Alteryx,
Looker, Qubole, Matillion, and Tableau. For a current list of the Snowflake
third-party partners, please visit the Snowflake web site at `https://docs.`
`snowflake.net/manuals/user-guide/ecosystem-all.html`.

Creating a Snowflake Account

Now you should be ready to create your Snowflake account, and this is
probably the easiest part of the whole process. If you do not have an account
yet, you can sign up online for a free trial. When logging into `www.snowflake.`
`com`, you should see the screen shown in Figure 2-1. The information that
was gathered in our planning stage will help us go through this quickly.
Click Start for Free in the upper-right corner of the page. This will give you a
30-day trial of Snowflake plus 400 Snowflake credits to play with.

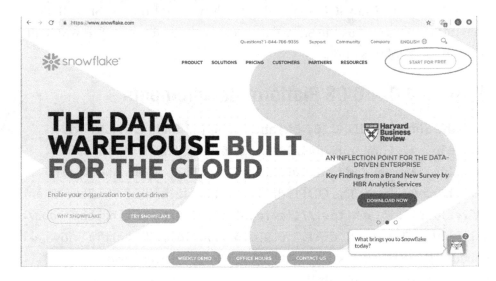

Figure 2-1. *Snowflake main web page*

Enter the following required details: name, company name, e-mail, phone number, Snowflake edition, cloud provider, and region. Finish by clicking Create Account, and in about 15 minutes, you will receive an e-mail with a link to your web interface. Figure 2-2 shows a sample e-mail. You must activate your account before going to the web interface.

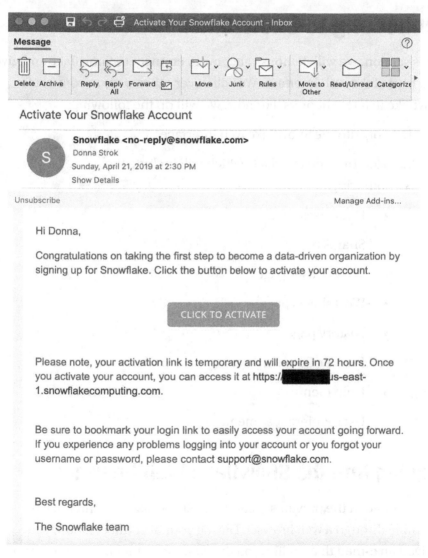

Figure 2-2. *E-mail received from Snowflake once account is provisioned*

Note   Account activation must occur within 72 hours or you will need to create another trial account.

Connecting to Snowflake

In this section, we will demonstrate how to connect to Snowflake and give you a tour of the web interface. We will cover other ways to connect to Snowflake in later chapters. For now, we will do the following:

1. Log into the Snowflake web interface

2. Tour the web interface, which will include the following:

   - Databases page

   - Shares page

   - Warehouses page

   - Worksheets page

   - History page

   - Partner Connect page

   - Help menu

   - User Preferences menu

Logging Into the Snowflake Web Interface

As mentioned in the previous section, the Snowflake web interface is accessible through a web browser. During your account creation, you received an e-mail that notifies you that your account has been provisioned.

This e-mail contains a link to your Snowflake web interface and a link to activate your account. Clicking Activate will take you to a web browser screen where you will be prompted to create a username and password. Once you have entered your desired username and password, the Welcome to Snowflake web interface will appear, as shown in Figure 2-3. Congratulations, you have officially logged into Snowflake!

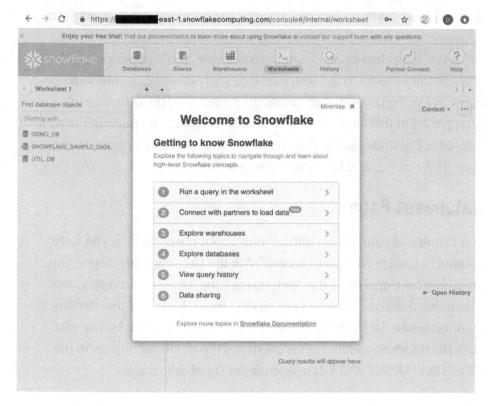

Figure 2-3. *Welcome to Snowflake screen*

Snowflake makes it easy to navigate and learn about the different features included in the web interface. We will go over what is included in the web interface in the next section.

Touring the Web Interface

Now that you've logged into your Snowflake web interface, you can create and manage all of your Snowflake objects. You can also use the web interface to load some data into tables, execute ad hoc queries, run Data Manipulation Language (DML) statements such as update, run Data Definition Language (DDL) statements such as alter/create, view past queries, change your password, set your user preferences, and perform administrative tasks if you've been granted admin access.

If you have the required administrator role, you can perform administrative tasks in the web interface such as creating and managing users. We will go over the administrative portion of the interface in Chapter 7. For this section, we will review the following parts of the web interface: Databases page, Warehouses page, Worksheets page, History page, Help menu, and User Preferences menu.

Databases Page

The Databases page shows information about the databases you have created or have privileges to access. With the necessary privileges, you are able to perform tasks that include creating, cloning, dropping, and modifying database objects; loading data into tables; and transferring ownership of a database to a different role. To do these tasks, you just click the database name. Figure 2-4 shows the database objects in the SNOWFLAKE_SAMPLE_DATA database on the Databases page.

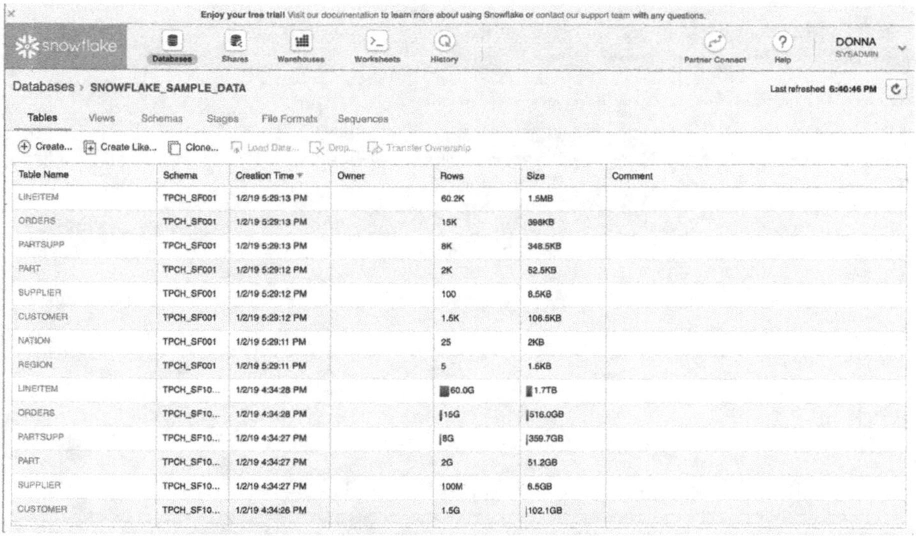

Figure 2-4. Snowflake's Databases page in the web user interface

Warehouses Page

The Warehouses page displays information about your virtual warehouses that have been created or that you have privileges to access. The administrative tasks that can be performed on virtual warehouses through this page include the following: creating or dropping, suspending or resuming, configuring, and transferring ownership to a different role. Figure 2-5 shows the virtual warehouses available in our example.

Figure 2-5. *Snowflake's Warehouses page*

Shares Page

If you need to share your data with other teams inside or outside your
organization, then Snowflake data sharing might be the solution you are
looking for. Snowflake data sharing enables data providers to effectively share
their data and to service their data consumers in a scalable and cost-effective
manner. Snowflake data sharing is available to all Snowflake customers.

Worksheets Page

The Worksheets page is probably going to be the most used page for those
with access to the Snowflake user interface. This page is where users can
submit ad hoc SQL queries and execute DDL and DML statements. Other
tasks that can be done on the Worksheets page include the following: opening
concurrent worksheets that work in separate sessions, saving and reopening
worksheets, logging out of Snowflake or switching roles within the worksheet,
exporting query results, and resizing the current virtual warehouse if needed.

Caution   If you log out of Snowflake, all running queries in the worksheet will cease.

History Page

The History page saves details of what was executed through the Worksheets page, SnowSQL, and any other SQL client that connects to your Snowflake instance. The history goes back 14 days, and you are able to view the details about each query. Results of queries are available for only 24 hours after the query has completed running. There are filters available to easily scan through the history, and you're also able to change how the history is viewed by adding additional columns, such as for the status or virtual warehouse.

Partner Connect Page

The Partner Connect page is available to the right of the History page. This page provides instant access to all the third-party partners that Snowflake is compatible with. It is easy to get set up; just click Partner Connect, choose the partner tool, and click Connect. Once you receive confirmation that your account was created, click Launch. In just a few short minutes you will be able to integrate the partner with your Snowflake account.

Help Menu

The Help menu is available in the upper-right corner of the Snowflake web interface, next to Partner Connect. The Help menu is where you can access the Snowflake documentation. Additionally, if you need support, the Help menu is where you can create a support case. Also, Snowflake drivers are available for download in the Help menu.

User Preferences Menu

The User Preferences menu can be accessed by clicking the drop-down menu in the upper-right corner, next to your account name. The preferences menu is where you can change your password, security role, and notification settings. It is also where you can log out of Snowflake.

Reminder   Logging out of Snowflake will cancel all running queries that are in a worksheet.

Summary

In this chapter, we covered planning your Snowflake environment and creating a Snowflake account, and we gave you a high-level overview of the web user interface. You are now ready to load data and build your virtual warehouse. The next few chapters will help you get started onboarding your data, and then later chapters will discuss the tools you can use to analyze your data.

## CHAPTER 3

Building a Virtual Warehouse

A Snowflake virtual warehouse is a cluster of compute resources for your Snowflake database. These compute resources include CPU, memory allocation, and temporary storage. Virtual warehouse concepts are important to understand because a virtual warehouse is the foundation of what you will build inside your Snowflake account. In this chapter, we will cover the following:

- Overview of Snowflake virtual data warehouses
- Understanding warehouse use cases
- Virtual data warehouse considerations
- Building your first Snowflake virtual data warehouse

Overview of Snowflake Virtual Warehouses

In this section, we will cover the different warehouse types and strategies for keeping costs down. The following are the topics that will be covered:

- Warehouse sizing and features
- Multicluster warehouses

© Dmitry Anoshin, Dmitry Shirokov, Donna Strok 2020
D. Anoshin et al., *Jumpstart Snowflake*, https://doi.org/10.1007/978-1-4842-5328-1_3

Warehouse Sizes and Features

Snowflake virtual warehouse sizes (as mentioned in Chapter 2) are T-shirt sizes such as X-Small, Small, Medium, Large, and so on. The credit charges for a virtual warehouse start at 1 for X-Small and double each size you go up. This makes it an easy pricing model to remember.

Choosing the Right Size

Even with the simple pricing model, it still might seem like a daunting task to come up with the approximate size needed for your virtual warehouse. Data loading and query processing are the two considerations that need to be mapped out when determining the size you need. As queries get more complex, the time it takes for the server to execute can increase. Likewise, as more data gets loaded into Snowflake, the loading performance might be affected.

Note   Larger virtual warehouses may not result in better performance for data loading or query processing.

Concurrency

The number of queries that a virtual warehouse can concurrently process is determined by the size and complexity of each query. As queries are submitted, the virtual warehouse calculates and reserves the compute resources needed to process each query. If the virtual warehouse does not have enough remaining resources to process a query, the query is queued, pending resources that become available as other running queries complete.

Snowflake provides some object-level parameters that can be set to help control query processing and concurrency.

- STATEMENT_QUEUED_TIMEOUT_IN_SECONDS
- STATEMENT_TIMEOUT_IN_SECONDS

Note   If queries are queuing more than desired, another virtual warehouse can be created, and queries can be manually redirected to the new virtual warehouse. In addition, resizing a virtual warehouse can enable limited scaling for query concurrency and queuing; however, virtual warehouse resizing is primarily for improving query performance.

To enable fully automated scaling for concurrency, Snowflake recommends multicluster virtual warehouses, which provide essentially the same benefits as creating additional virtual warehouses and redirecting queries but without requiring manual intervention. Multicluster virtual warehouses are discussed later in this chapter.

Default Virtual Warehouses in Sessions

When a session is initiated in Snowflake, the session does not, by default, have a virtual warehouse associated with it. Until a session has a virtual warehouse associated with it, queries cannot be submitted within the session. Snowflake allows sessions to specify which virtual warehouse they will default to. Sessions can be initiated by users or tools, and sessions may also change to another virtual warehouse by using the USE WAREHOUSE command.

To facilitate querying immediately after a session is initiated, Snowflake supports specifying a default virtual warehouse for each individual user. The default warehouse for a user is used as the warehouse for all sessions initiated by that user. A default warehouse can be specified when creating or modifying the user, either by using the web interface or by using CREATE USER/ALTER USER.

Snowflake clients (SnowSQL, JDBC driver, ODBC driver, Python connector, etc.) can specify a default warehouse through their connections or configuration files, as appropriate. Chapters 4, 5, and 6 discuss these Snowflake clients and provide more information on how to set up the default warehouse.

Multicluster Virtual Warehouses

Some organizations may replicate data into separate data marts. They may also shift some data workloads outside of normal business hours or queue usage to boost performance. Snowflake offers users the ability to automatically scale out their virtual warehouse by distributing replicated data, in memory, across separate compute clusters.

Resizing your virtual warehouse can provide performance benefits for slow-running queries and data loading. Multicluster warehouses will automatically increase or decrease the number of queries.

Multicluster virtual warehouses are an Enterprise Edition feature. If multicluster virtual warehouses are enabled for your account, you can also set the maximum and minimum number of clusters for the warehouse. Multicluster warehouses will use multiple clusters of servers to handle cases where fluctuating numbers of concurrent queries occur, such as during peak and off-peak hours. As the load increases, the virtual warehouse automatically starts more clusters to prevent queries from queuing. When the additional clusters are no longer needed, it shuts them down.

Note   Multicluster virtual warehouses are a Snowflake Enterprise Edition feature.

Overview of Multicluster Virtual Warehouses

Multicluster virtual warehouses improve concurrency and are designed specifically for handling queuing and performance issues related to large numbers of concurrent queries by many users. In addition, multicluster virtual warehouses can be automated to scale if your number of users/queries tends to fluctuate.

When deciding whether to use multicluster virtual warehouses and the number of clusters to use per virtual warehouse, consider the following:

- All your virtual warehouses should be configured as multicluster virtual warehouses.

- Multicluster virtual warehouses should be configured to run in autoscaling mode, which enables Snowflake to automatically start and stop clusters as needed.

When choosing the minimum and maximum number of clusters for a multicluster warehouse, consider the following:

- **Minimum**: Keep the default value of 1; this ensures that additional clusters are started only as needed. However, if high availability of the virtual warehouse is a concern, set the value higher than 1. This helps ensure virtual warehouse availability and continuity in the unlikely event that a cluster fails.

- **Maximum**: Set this value as large as possible, while being mindful of the virtual warehouse size and corresponding credit costs. For example, an X-Large virtual warehouse (16 servers) with maximum clusters (10) will consume 160 credits in an hour if all 10 clusters run continuously for the hour.

Multicluster Credits and Usage

To see your consumption in the web interface, click the name of a warehouse to display the average load on the warehouse for all queries processed and queued over the last two weeks. The page displays the query load in intervals of five minutes or one hour depending on the length of the viewing window. Each time a virtual warehouse is resumed or increases in size, your account is billed for one minute of usage; after the first minute, billing is calculated per second. Figure 3-1 shows what the usage screen looks like.

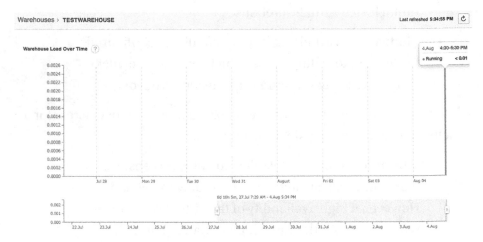

Figure 3-1. *A newly created virtual warehouse's load over time*

Credits are charged based on the following:

- The number of servers per cluster, which is determined by the virtual warehouse size

- The number of clusters, if using multicluster virtual warehouses

- The length of time each server in each cluster runs

Virtual Warehouse Considerations

While reading this book, you may be looking for a solution for your use case. Typical virtual warehouse design considerations include the following:

- Query design

- Query caching, reuse of frequently run queries

- Scaling

Query Design

The number of servers required to process a query depends on the size and complexity of the query. Queries will scale linearly as a virtual warehouse size increases, particularly for larger, more complex queries. Therefore, consider the following in your query design:

- Table size is more significant than the number of rows.

- Filters using predicates impact processing.

- A higher number of joins will also impact processing.

Tip   To achieve the best results, try to execute relatively homogeneous queries (size, complexity, data sets, etc.) on the same warehouse; executing queries of widely varying size and/or complexity on the same warehouse makes it more difficult to analyze warehouse load, which can make it more difficult to select the best size to match the size, composition, and number of queries in your workload.

Caching Impacts

When a virtual warehouse is in a running state, it maintains a cache of table data that has been accessed from previously completed queries. The size of the cache is determined by the number of servers in the virtual warehouse. The size of the cache increases as the virtual warehouse size increases.

The cache is dropped when the virtual warehouse is suspended, which may result in slower initial performance for some queries as the virtual warehouse is resumed. The cache is rebuilt when a warehouse is resumed, and queries are then able to take advantage of the improved performance that the cache provides.

Consider the trade-off between saving credits by suspending a virtual warehouse versus maintaining the cache of data from previous queries to help with performance.

Scaling

Virtual warehouse resizing is supported by Snowflake at any time. You can even resize a warehouse while the virtual warehouse is running. When you have a slow query and have other similarly sized queries queued up, it might make sense to resize the warehouse while it's running.

But be aware that larger is not necessarily faster; for smaller, basic queries that are already executing quickly, you may not see any significant improvement after resizing. If a query is already running, then it will not be impacted by the resized virtual warehouse. The additional virtual warehouses will be used only by the queued or new queries that will be processed.

Building a Snowflake Virtual Warehouse

There are two ways you can build a Snowflake virtual warehouse. It can be done either through the web interface or through SQL commands. We will demonstrate how to do it in both ways. We will be doing this through an already created Snowflake account. If you haven't yet created your Snowflake account, please review Chapter 2 to get your Snowflake account set up. Let's get started!

Creating a Virtual Warehouse

SNOWFLAKE WEB INTERFACE

1. Log in to your Snowflake web interface.

2. Click Warehouses + Create.

3. Give your virtual warehouse a name, choose a size, and set the maximum idle time before the virtual warehouse automatically suspends. Click Finish. Figure 3-2 shows this information entered into the web interface.

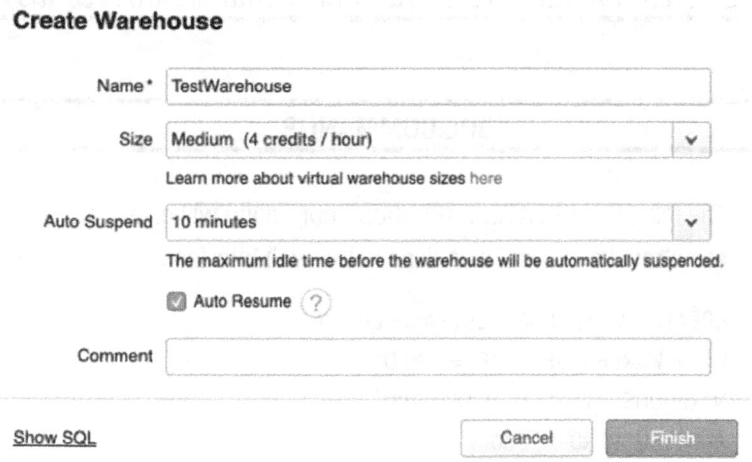

Create Warehouse

Name*	TestWarehouse
Size	Medium (4 credits / hour)
	Learn more about virtual warehouse sizes here
Auto Suspend	10 minutes
	The maximum idle time before the warehouse will be automatically suspended.
	☑ Auto Resume ⑦
Comment	

Show SQL   Cancel   Finish

Figure 3-2. *Create Warehouse dialog in web interface after selecting Create Warehouse*

Tip   After entering the details, click Show SQL at the bottom of the Create Warehouse dialog to see the SQL that would perform this same task. Figure 3-3 shows what this would look like based on the setup in Figure 3-2.

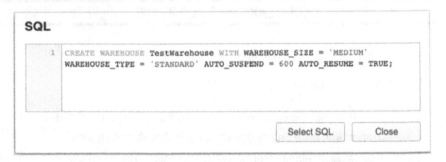

Figure 3-3. *Show SQL will display the SQL code that can be used in a script. In this example, AUTO_SUSPEND automatically translates the minutes entered into the Create Warehouse dialog into seconds*

SQL COMMANDS

1. The following CREATE WAREHOUSE command will give the same results as what was done in the web interface:

    ```
    CREATE WAREHOUSE TestWarehouse
    WITH WAREHOUSE_SIZE = 'MEDIUM'
    WAREHOUSE_TYPE = 'STANDARD'
    AUTO_SUSPEND = 600
    AUTO_RESUME = TRUE;
    ```

2. Figure 3-4 shows that our warehouse, TESTWAREHOUSE, is created after provisioning was completed.

Status	Warehouse Name	Size	Run...	Que...	Auto Suspend	Auto Re
Started	TESTWAREHOUSE	Medium	0	0	10 minutes	Yes
Suspended	COMPUTE_WH	X-Large	0	0	10 minutes	Yes

Figure 3-4. *TESTWAREHOUSE has completed provisioning and is now appearing in our list of warehouses*

Important   Always ensure that auto suspend and auto resume are set in your warehouse. By default, these settings are set for you when a virtual warehouse is provisioned. Auto suspend stops a warehouse if it sits idle for a specified period of time, while auto resume starts a suspended virtual warehouse when queries are submitted to it. This is important because a running warehouse will consume Snowflake credits only when compute resources are being utilized. Shutting down your warehouse, when they are not in use, will help conserve credits and control costs.

Starting, Resuming, Suspending, and Resizing

You can also manually start/resume, suspend, and resize a virtual warehouse. These are especially helpful for one-offs or if you don't want to wait for the automatic start or suspension of your virtual warehouse. A virtual warehouse can be started at any time, even when it's first created.

WEB INTERFACE

Here are the steps for common tasks:

- **Start/Resume**: Click Warehouses and select your warehouse. Click Resume.

- **Suspend**: Click Warehouses and select your warehouse. Click Suspend.

- **Resize**: Click Warehouses and select your warehouse. Click Configure. Select the new size from the Size drop-down. Click Finish.

SQL COMMAND

Here are commands for common tasks:

- **Start/Resume**: Use the ALTER WAREHOUSE command with RESUME.

  ```
  ALTER WAREHOUSE TestWarehouse
  RESUME IF SUSPENDED
  ```

- **Suspend**: Use the ALTER WAREHOUSE command with SUSPEND.

  ```
  ALTER WAREHOUSE TestWarehouse
  SUSPEND
  ```

- **Resize**: Use the ALTER WAREHOUSE command with SET WAREHOUSE_SIZE.

  ```
  ALTER WAREHOUSE TestWarehouse
  SET WAREHOUSE_SIZE = XSMALL
  ```

Using a Warehouse

The USE WAREHOUSE command is used only as a SQL command. This simply allows the SQL statements to connect to the correct virtual warehouse during execution. When using the Worksheets page in the web interface, the USE WAREHOUSE command is implied by selecting the virtual warehouse at the top right of the screen, as shown in Figure 3-5.

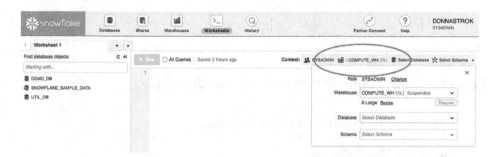

Figure 3-5. *This shows how to view or change the virtual warehouse within the worksheet*

Setting Up Load Monitoring

The load monitoring dashboard is used for the performance monitoring of your virtual warehouses within your account. There is also a feature of the dashboard that lets you monitor your credits over a period of time. Log into your Snowflake web interface to begin setting up load monitoring.

1. Click Warehouses and highlight your chosen warehouse. A page will appear on the right allowing you to grant privileges.

2. Click Grant Privileges.

3. For "Privileges to grant," select MONITOR.

4. For "Grant privileges to," select ACCOUNTADMIN.

5. Click Grant, as shown in Figure 3-6.

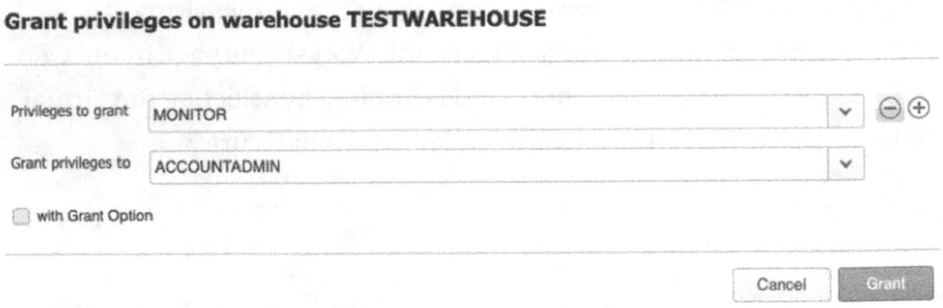

Grant privileges on warehouse TESTWAREHOUSE

Privileges to grant   MONITOR

Grant privileges to   ACCOUNTADMIN

☐ with Grant Option

Cancel   Grant

Figure 3-6. *The information entered into the dialog*

To view load monitoring, do the following:

1. Click Warehouses.

2. Click your choice of warehouse name (which should be hyperlinked).

Figure 3-7 shows how the loading monitoring chart looks on a newly created warehouse. There is one bar at the end of the Warehouse Load Over Time chart, because we ran one query. At the bottom there is a date slider that allows you to increase or decrease the date range you want to see in the chart. There is no history in this chart; therefore, no more bars appear.

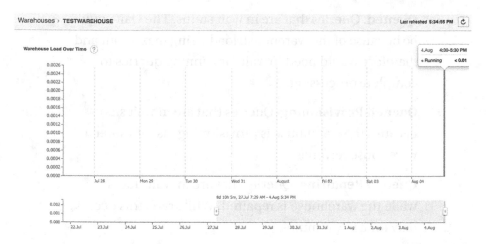

Figure 3-7. *Warehouse Load Over Time chart on the TestWarehouse warehouse*

Note   The date slider has a minimum/maximum range of 8 hours to 14 days. Load monitoring data is not available previous to 14 days.

Understanding Load Monitoring

The Warehouse Load Over Time bar chart contains bars that represent time intervals. Each bar, or interval, represents the query loads that are based on query statuses for the queries executing or queuing at that time. There are four types of query statuses: Running, Queued, Queued Provisioning, and Queued Repairing.

- **Running**: Queries that were actively running during the interval. These queries may have started before or during the interval.

- **Queued**: Queries that are in wait status. The wait could be because of the warehouse load being maxed out and therefore would need to wait for running queries to complete processing.

- **Queued Provisioning**: Queries that are in wait status because the warehouse is provisioning, usually after a warehouse resumes.

- **Queued Repairing**: Queries that are in wait status while the warehouse is repaired. While rare, this occurs only for a few minutes.

Query load is calculated by taking the execution time for each query and dividing it by the interval time in seconds. This produces a percent that is then additive for all the queries in that interval. The percent is divided up by query status, which is displayed in the bar chart.

Best Practices for Load Monitoring

These are some best practices for load monitoring:

- A high query load and queuing are indicative of needing to start up a separate warehouse. Move the queued queries to the new warehouse.

- A low query load could mean your running queries need more compute resources. Resizing the warehouse can take care of this.

- Use the load monitor to study how the daily workloads look over the course of two weeks. Notice the trends in spikes and consider creating a warehouse specifically for peak workloads. Or consider switching to multicluster so that autoscaling takes care of the peak traffic.

- Use the load monitor to look at trends in Snowflake credit usages. See whether the minimum cluster count or warehouse size needs to be decreased to save money on credits.

Summary

This chapter covered the basics of Snowflake virtual warehouses. You should now know the different virtual warehouse sizes and features and what a multicluster virtual warehouse is. We also reviewed some important things to consider with your virtual warehouse. Last, we showed how to create your first virtual warehouse and highlighted the load monitoring tool.

CHAPTER 4

Loading Bulk Data into Snowflake

There are two ways to load data into Snowflake: bulk data loading with the COPY statement and continuous data loading with Snowpipe. This chapter is focused on bulk data loading. We will cover the following topics:

- **Overview of bulk data loading**: We will cover what bulk data loading is, file load locations, supported file formats and encoding, compression handling, and encryption options.

- **Bulk data loading recommendations**: We will cover file preparation including file sizing and splitting, the CSV and semistructured formats, staging, loading, and querying.

Note Continuous data loading with Snowpipe is covered in Chapter 6.

© Dmitry Anoshin, Dmitry Shirokov, Donna Strok 2020
D. Anoshin et al., *Jumpstart Snowflake*, https://doi.org/10.1007/978-1-4842-5328-1_4

Overview of Bulk Data Loading

The bulk loading of data using COPY has been done longer than Snowflake has been around. Many other database management systems support using the COPY statement. Therefore, it is no surprise that Snowflake offers the same support. To better understand bulk data loading, we will review and answer these key questions:

- What is bulk data loading?

- Where can we bulk data load from?

- What are the compression and encryption options?

- What file formats are supported?

What Is Bulk Data Loading?

To get data into a database table, you need to insert it. Insert statements can take a while since they need to be executed one row at a time. Bulk copying can take a large amount of data and insert it into a database all in one batch. The bulk data loading option in Snowflake allows batch loading of data from files that are in cloud storage, like AWS S3.

If your data files are not currently in cloud storage, then there is an option to copy the data files from a local machine to a cloud storage *staging area* before loading them into Snowflake. This is known as Snowflake's *internal* staging area. The data files are transmitted from a local machine to an internal, Snowflake-designated, cloud storage staging location and then loaded into tables using the COPY command.

Tip   External tables can be created instead of loading data into Snowflake. This would be useful when only a portion of data is needed.

Bulk Load Locations

Snowflake supports loading data from files staged in any of the following cloud storage locations, regardless of the cloud platform for your Snowflake account:

- Snowflake-designated internal storage staging location

- AWS S3, where files can be loaded directly from any user-supplied S3 bucket

- GCP Cloud Storage, where files can be loaded directly from any user-supplied GCP Cloud Storage container

- Azure Blob storage, where files can be loaded directly from any user-supplied Azure container

---

Note   Data transfer billing charges may apply when loading data from files staged across different platforms. Refer to Chapter 2 for more information.

Supported File Formats and Encoding

Snowflake supports most of the common file formats used for loading data. These file formats include the following:

- Delimited files (any valid delimiter is supported; the default is a comma)

- JSON and XML

- Avro, including the automatic detection and processing of staged Avro files that were compressed using Snappy

- ORC, including the automatic detection and processing of staged ORC files that were compressed using Snappy or zlib

55

- Parquet, including the automatic detection and processing of staged Parquet files that were compressed using Snappy

For delimited files, the default character set is UTF-8. To use any other characters set, you must explicitly specify the encoding to use for loading. For all other supported file formats (JSON, Avro, etc.), the only supported character set is UTF-8.

Note   Many character encoding sets are supported for the loading of delimited files. Refer to Snowflake's online documentation for more details on which character encodings are supported.

Snowflake also allows you to configure a file format object for reuse. This can be done through the user interface or with SQL code. This is useful for formats that are frequently used by many load jobs. Here is an example of a file format named "DEMO_DB"."PUBLIC".sample_file_format. The file format object name can then be referenced during the bulk load command.

```
CREATE FILE FORMAT "DEMO_DB"."PUBLIC".sample_file_format
TYPE = 'CSV' COMPRESSION = 'AUTO' FIELD_DELIMITER = ',' RECORD_
DELIMITER = '\n' SKIP_HEADER = 0 FIELD_OPTIONALLY_ENCLOSED_BY =
'NONE' TRIM_SPACE = FALSE ERROR_ON_COLUMN_COUNT_MISMATCH = TRUE
ESCAPE = 'NONE' ESCAPE_UNENCLOSED_FIELD = '\134' DATE_FORMAT =
'AUTO' TIMESTAMP_FORMAT = 'AUTO' NULL_IF = ('\\N');
```

Compression Handling

When staging uncompressed files in a Snowflake stage, the files are automatically compressed using gzip, unless compression is explicitly disabled. Snowflake can automatically the detect gzip, bzip2, deflate, and `raw_deflate` compression methods. Autodetection is not yet supported for `brotli` and `zstandard`. Therefore, when staging or loading files compressed with either of these methods, you must explicitly specify the compression method that was used.

Encryption Options

When staging unencrypted files in an internal Snowflake location, the files are automatically encrypted using 128-bit keys. 256-bit keys can be enabled (for stronger encryption); however, additional configuration is required. Files that are already encrypted can be loaded into Snowflake from external cloud storage; the key used to encrypt the files must be provided to Snowflake.

Bulk Data Loading Recommendations

Loading large data sets can affect query performance. Snowflake recommends dedicating separate warehouses to loading and querying operations to optimize the performance for each. In this section, we will cover the recommended ways to prepare the files.

File Preparation

The number of data files that can be processed in parallel is determined by the number and capacity of servers in a warehouse. If you follow the file sizing guidelines described in the following section, the data loading will require minimal resources. Note that these recommendations apply to both bulk data loads and continuous loading using Snowpipe.

File Sizing

Know the following about file sizing:

- The number of load operations that can run in parallel cannot exceed the number of data files to be loaded.

- To optimize the number of parallel operations for a load, we recommend aiming to produce data files roughly 10 MB to 100 MB in size, compressed.

- Aggregate smaller files to minimize the processing overhead for each file.

- Split larger files into a greater number of smaller files to distribute the load among the servers in an active warehouse. The number of data files processed in parallel is determined by the number and capacity of servers in a warehouse.

- Snowflake recommends splitting large files by line to avoid records that span chunks.

- Data loads of large Parquet files (e.g., greater than 3 GB) could time out. Split large files into files 1 GB in size (or smaller) for loading.

File Splitting

If your source database does not allow you to export data files in smaller chunks, use a third-party utility to split large CSV files. Windows does not include a native file split utility; however, Windows supports many third-party tools and scripts that can split large data files. Linux has the `split` utility, which enables you to split a CSV file into multiple smaller files.

Note   Splitting larger data files allows the load to scale linearly. Using a larger warehouse (X-Large, 2X-Large, etc.) will consume more credits and may not result in any performance increase.

CSV File Preparation

Consider the following guidelines when preparing your delimited text (CSV) files for loading:

- UTF-8 is the default character set; however, additional encodings are supported. Use the ENCODING file format option to specify the character set for the data files.

- Snowflake supports ASCII characters (including high-order characters) as delimiters. Common field delimiters include the pipe (|), comma (,), caret (^), and tilde (~).

- A field can be optionally enclosed by double quotes, and, within the field, all special characters are automatically escaped, except the double quote itself needs to be escaped by having two double quotes right next to each other (""). For unenclosed fields, a backslash (\) is the default escape character.

- Common escape sequences can be used (e.g., \t for tab, \n for newline, \r for carriage return, and \\ for backslash).

- Fields containing carriage returns should also be enclosed in quotes (single or double).

- The number of columns in each row should be consistent.

Semistructured Data File Preparation

Semistructured data is data that does not conform to the standards of traditional structured data, but it contains tags or other types of markup that identify individual, distinct entities within the data.

Two of the key attributes that distinguish semistructured data from structured data are nested data structures and the lack of a fixed schema.

- Structured data requires a fixed schema that is defined before the data can be loaded and queried in a relational database system. Semistructured data does not require a prior definition of a schema and can constantly evolve; i.e., new attributes can be added at any time.

- In addition, entities within the same class may have different attributes even though they are grouped together, and the order of the attributes is not important.

- Unlike structured data, which represents data as a flat table, semistructured data can contain n level of hierarchies of nested information.

The steps for loading semistructured data into tables are identical to those for loading structured data into relational tables. Snowflake loads semistructured data into a single `VARIANT` column. You can also use a `COPY INTO` table statement during data transformation to extract selected columns from a staged data file into separate table columns.

When semistructured data is inserted into a `VARIANT` column, what Snowflake is really doing is extracting information about the key locations and values and saving it into a semistructured document. The document is referenced by the metadata engine for fast SQL retrieval.

Note   VARIANT "null" values (not to be confused with SQL NULL values) are not loaded to the table. To avoid this, extract semistructured data elements containing "null" values into relational columns before loading them, Alternatively, if the "null" values in your files indicate missing values and have no other special meaning, Snowflake recommends setting the file format option STRIP_NULL_VALUES to TRUE when loading the semistructured data files.

File Staging

Both internal and external stage locations in Snowflake can include a path (referred to as a *prefix* in AWS). When staging regular data sets, Snowflake recommends partitioning the data into logical paths to identify details such as geographical location, along with the date, when the data is written.

Organizing your data files by path allows you to copy the data into Snowflake with a single command. This allows you to execute concurrent COPY statements that match a subset of files, taking advantage of parallel operations.

For example, if you were storing data for a company that did business all over the world, you might include identifiers such as continent, country, and city in paths along with data write dates. Here are two examples:

- NA/Mexico/Quintana_Roo/Cancun/2020/01/01/01/

- EU/France/Paris/2020/01/01/05/

When you create a named stage, you can specify any part of a path. For example, create an external stage using one of the previous example paths:

```
create stage test_stage url='s3://bucketname/united_states/
washington/seattle/' credentials=(aws_key_id='1234lkj'
aws_secret_key='asdlj1234');
```

You can also add a path when you stage files in an internal user or table stage. For example, you can stage `mydata.csv` in a specific path in the `t1` table stage with this:

```
put file:///local/myfile.csv @%t1/united_states/washington/
seattle/2020/01/01/01/
```

When loading your staged data, narrow the path to the most granular level that includes your data for improved data load performance.

- If the file names match except for a suffix or extension, include the matching part of the file names in the path. Here's an example:

  ```
  copy into t1 from @%t1/united_states/washington/
  seattle/2020/01/01/01/myfile;
  ```

- Add the `FILES` or `PATTERN` option. Here's an example:

  - ```
    copy into t1 from @%t1/united_states/
    california/los_angeles/2016/06/01/11/
    files=('mydata1.csv', 'mydata1.csv');
    ```

  - ```
    copy into t1 from @%t1/united_states/
    california/los_angeles/2016/06/01/11/
    pattern='.*mydata[^[0-9]{1,3}$$].csv';
    ```

When planning regular data loads, such as with extract-transform-load (ETL) processing, it is important to partition the data in your internal (i.e., Snowflake) stage or external locations (S3 buckets or Azure containers) using logical, granular paths. Create a partitioning structure that includes identifying details such as the application or location, along with the date when the data was written. You can then copy any fraction of the partitioned data into Snowflake with a single command. You can copy data into Snowflake by the hour, day, month, or even year when you initially populate tables.

Here are some examples of partitioned S3 buckets using paths:

- `s3://bucket_name/brand/2016/07/01/11/`

- `s3://bucket_name/region/country/2016/07/01/14/`

Note   S3 transmits a directory list with each COPY statement used by Snowflake, so reducing the number of files in each directory improves the performance of your COPY statements.

Loading

The COPY command supports several options for loading data files from a stage.

- By path of internal location or prefix of external location
- By listing specific files to load (up to 1,000 per COPY command)
- By using pattern matching to identify specific files by pattern

These options enable you to copy a fraction of the staged data into a Snowflake table with a single command. This allows you to execute concurrent COPY statements that match a subset of files, taking advantage of parallel operations. Do take special note that the file being copied must have the same data structure (i.e., number of columns, data type) as the table.

Tip   Listing specific files to load from a stage is generally the fastest.

Here's an example of a list of files:

```
copy into sample_table from @%sample_data/data1/ files=
('sample_file1.csv', 'sample_file2.csv', 'sample_file3.csv')
```

Here's a pattern matching example:

```
copy into sample_table from @%sample_data/data1/
pattern='.*sample_file[^0-9{1,3}$$].csv';
```

In general, pattern matching using a regular expression is the slowest of the three options for identifying/specifying data files to load from a stage; however, this option works well if you exported your files in named order from your external application and want to batch load the files in the same order. Pattern matching can be combined with paths for further control over data loading.

When data from staged files is loaded successfully, consider removing the staged files to ensure the data isn't inadvertently loaded again (duplicated). Staged files can be deleted from a Snowflake stage (user stage, table stage, or named stage) using the following methods:

- Files that were loaded successfully can be deleted from the stage during a load by specifying the PURGE copy option in the COPY INTO <table> command.

- After the load completes, use the REMOVE command to remove the files in the stage.

Querying Staged Files

Snowflake automatically generates metadata for files in Snowflake's internal file staging or external (i.e., AWS S3, Google Cloud Storage, or Microsoft Azure) file staging. This metadata can be queried with the following:

- A standard SELECT statement.

- During a COPY into a table. Transformations may be applied to the columns in the same SELECT statement.

Note   Querying is primarily for performing simple queries during
the data loading only and is not intended to replace querying already
loaded tables.

Here's the query syntax for a standard SELECT statement:

```
SELECT [<alias>.]$<file_col_num>[.<element>] [ ,
[<alias>.]$<file_col_num>[.<element>] , ...   ]
  FROM { <internal_location> | <external_location> }
  [ ( FILE_FORMAT => <namespace>.<named_file_format> ) ]
  [ <alias> ]
```

Here's the query syntax during a load:

```
/* Data load with transformation */
COPY INTO [<namespace>.]<table_name> [ ( <col_name> [ ,
<col_name> ... ] ) ]
    FROM ( SELECT [<alias>.]$<file_col_num>[.<element>] [ ,
    [<alias>.]$<file_col_num>[.<element>] ... ]
        FROM { internalStage | externalStage } )
```

Bulk Loading with the Snowflake Web Interface

For smaller files (less than 50 MB), loading from the Snowflake web
interface is fine.

Note   If a file is large, then it should be loaded using SnowSQL or
Snowpipe. See the following chapters for more information on how to
bulk load with SnowSQL and Snowpipe.

BULK FILE LOADING THROUGH THE SNOWFLAKE USER INTERFACE

Prerequisites

1. You need a Snowflake account; please review Chapter 2 to set one up.

2. Download the file named `zips2000.csv`.

Instructions

1. Log into the Snowflake web user interface.

2. Click Databases + Tables.

3. Click Create Table and enter the values shown in Figure 4-1.

Figure 4-1. *Create Table dialog that allows you to enter a table name along with column names and their data types*

4. Click Load Data, and the Load Data wizard (Figure 4-2) will appear. Select the warehouse you want to use and click Next.

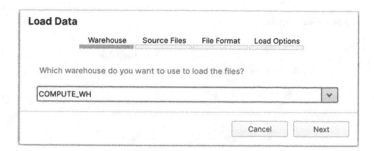

Figure 4-2. *The Load Data wizard will appear once you click Load Data*

5. Click Select Files to browse for `zips2000.csv` in the location you saved it in (Figure 4-3). Click Next.

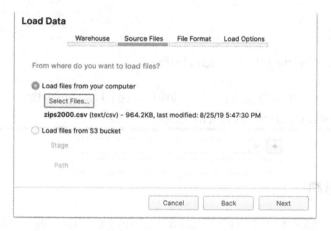

Figure 4-3. *Source files getting selected*

6. Click the Add (looks like a plus sign) button to add a file format. Enter what is shown in Figure 4-4. Click Finish.

Figure 4-4. *Create File Format dialog*

7. Click Load, and your table will load. Once it has completed loading, you can query it as usual.

Summary

In this chapter, we reviewed bulk data loading with COPY, and we covered what bulk data loading is, file load locations, supported file formats and encoding, compression handling, and encryption options. We also covered bulk data loading recommendations including file preparation and staging, loading, and querying. In addition, we went through some sample exercises on bulk loading data using COPY in our virtual warehouse.

CHAPTER 5

Getting Started with SnowSQL

SnowSQL is the next-generation command-line client for connecting to Snowflake, executing SQL queries, and performing all DDL and DML operations, including loading data into and unloading data out of database tables.

In this chapter, we will go over the following topics:

- Installing SnowSQL

- Configuring SnowSQL

- Using commands in SnowSQL

- Making multiple connections

- Loading data using SnowSQL

After this chapter, you will be able to load data into Snowflake using the SnowSQL command-line interface.

Installing SnowSQL

SnowSQL can be downloaded and installed from the Snowflake web site or from its various S3 URL locations. Refer to the Snowflake site for these URLs. All the required software for installing SnowSQL is bundled in the

© Dmitry Anoshin, Dmitry Shirokov, Donna Strok 2020
D. Anoshin et al., *Jumpstart Snowflake*, https://doi.org/10.1007/978-1-4842-5328-1_5

installers. Snowflake provides platform-specific versions of SnowSQL for download.

- **Microsoft Windows (64-bit)**: Windows 7 or higher, Windows Server 2008 R2 or higher

- **macOS**: v10.12 or higher

- **Linux (64-bit)**: CentOS 6 or higher, Ubuntu 14 or higher

For Homebrew enthusiasts, the Cask extension has an installation package available by executing the following: `brew cask install snowflake-snowsql`.

As with most installations, you must first download it and then install. This can be automated through scripting, which may be useful if deploying through a CI/CD process. In automation scenarios, you can use `curl` commands to download and then run the installations. There are several online locations available to download the software from. Check with the Snowflake online documentation for specific file names. For simplicity, we will walk you through how to install SnowSQL on macOS, version 10.14.2, using the download from the Snowflake web user interface. This is a great exercise for proof of concepts or ad hoc work performed on personal desktops. However, where possible, we will include Windows information in each step.

1. Log into the Snowflake web user interface. Click Help + Downloads. This brings up the Downloads dialog, which gives you all the options of the SnowSQL CLI client (Figure 5-1).

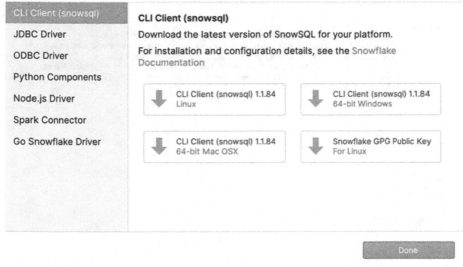

Figure 5-1. *Downloads dialog*

2. Download the version of the CLI client for SnowSQL
    that is appropriate for your operating system. For
    this demonstration, the CLI client for macOS will be
    downloaded.

3. Once the download is complete, double-click the
    downloaded application to begin the installation.
    The installation should open to the Install Snowflake
    SnowSQL dialog (Figure 5-2). Click Continue.

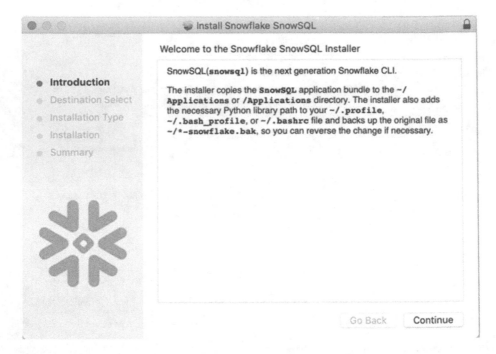

Figure 5-2. SnowSQL installation "introduction" screen

4.   Keep the installation's defaults unless you need to
     install it to a special location. Once the installation is
     complete, you should be on the Summary tab of the
     installation guide and should see the "Installation
     is Complete" message. You should also see some
     important information that needs to be followed
     after clicking Close (Figure 5-3). Make sure to keep
     this information handy. These steps will be covered
     in the section "Configuring SnowSQL."

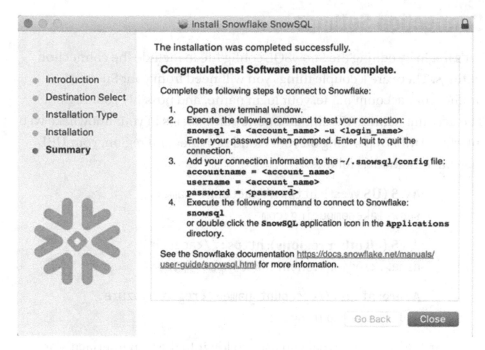

Figure 5-3. *The Install Snowflake SnowSQL wizard's Summary screen*

Configuring SnowSQL

Now that SnowSQL is successfully installed, we will review how to configure it. The configuration of SnowSQL takes place in the configuration file named `config`. There are three sections to the configuration file, which we will review in this section:

- Connection settings

- Configuration options

- Configuration variables

Connection Settings

Let's begin by editing the SnowSQL config file to include the connection settings. There are a couple things you will need from your Snowflake profile: your account name, your login name, and possibly your region. The account name is the alphanumeric value that is in your Snowflake web interface URL. Depending on your cloud provider and region, your URL may be formatted as follows:

> **AWS (US West)**: `https://<account_name>.snowflakecomputing.com`

> **AWS (all other regions)**: `https://<account_name>.<region>.snowflakecomputing.com`

> **Azure**: `https://<account_name>.<region>.azure.snowflakecomputing.com`

Your `login_name` is what you used to log into the web interface. For more information on Snowflake account names, please see Snowflake's online documentation at `https://docs.snowflake.net/manuals/user-guide/connecting.html`.

Note   The config file must be saved in UTF-8 encoding.

```
EDITING CONNECTION SETTINGS IN THE CONFIGURATION FILE
```

1. Open a new terminal window and execute the following command to test the connection to your Snowflake account:

    ```
    snowsql -a account_name -u login_name
    ```

    Here's an example:

    ```
    snowsql -a < xxx71531 -u DONNA
    ```

2. To save these credentials locally so that they do not need to
    be typed, edit the config file located in the ~/.snowsql/
    Linux folder or %USERPROFILE%\.snowsql\ in Windows. Edit
    the following values by uncommenting and saving the values
    pertaining to your account. Enclose the password in quotes if
    there are any special characters.

```
accountname = account_name
username = login_name
password = xxxxxxxx
region = region_code
```

Here's an example:

```
accountname = xxx71531
username = DONNA
password = xxxxxxxx
region = us-east-1
```

3. Test your credentials by opening a new terminal window and
    executing snowsql, as shown in Figure 5-4.

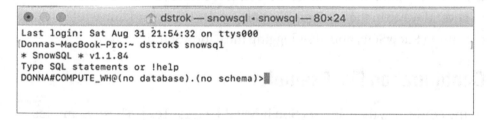

Figure 5-4. *Executing the snowsql command with all the credentials saved in the config file*

Caution   The password is stored in plain text in the config file. Alternatively, you can leave the password out of the config file and sign in every time. However, this will interfere with automation. Therefore, if leaving the password in the config file, the file must explicitly be secured to restrict access. In Linux or macOS, this can be performed by setting the read permissions to your own user by running the `chmod` command like this:

`chmod 700 ~/.snowsql/config`

Configuration Variables

Variables offer a chance to set default values to frequently accessed database objects or user-defined values. A variable is a string of alphanumeric (case-insensitive) characters representing the name of the variable. It may be enclosed in quotes, if needed. An example use case for a variable is setting the default date as the current date for queries or setting the default database to production. You can define variables for SnowSQL in several ways: in the configuration file, at the command line while executing SnowSQL, and after logging into SnowSQL.

Configuration File Example

In the config file, there is a section labeled `[variables]`. These examples will be using the sample database named `SNOWFLAKE_SAMPLE_DATA` preloaded to Snowflake when you create your account.

1. Open the config configuration file in a text editor. The default location of the file is as follows:

    Linux/macOS: `~/.snowsql/`
    Windows: `%USERPROFILE%\.snowsql\`

Tip   You can use a different location for the configuration file; just use -config followed by the path when starting up SnowSQL at the command line. Here's an example:

```
-config <path/to/config>
```

2. Locate the [variables] section and add the following text:

    ```
    database_name = SNOWFLAKE_SAMPLE_DATA
    schema_name = TPCH_SF001
    table_name = NATION
    ```

3. Save and close the config file. Test this by executing each of the following commands in a terminal window; the results should match Figure 5-5. Note that this will work only if the connection variables are set. See "Connection Settings" to set up your config file.

    ```
    snowsql
    !set variable_substitution=true
    USE "&database_name";
    USE SCHEMA "&schema_name";
    Select count(*) from "&table_name";
    !quit
    ```

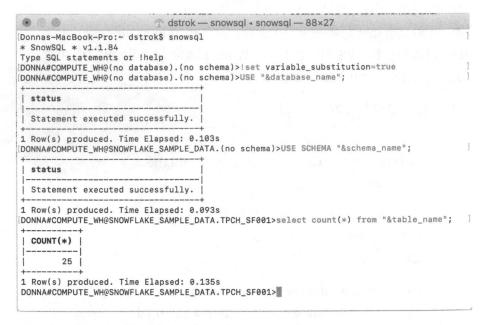

Figure 5-5. *The output of each command executed in SnowSQL. The variables are added in the config file and set with the command !set variable_substitution=true*

Command-Line Example

The same type of variable setting can be performed at the command line before being executed in SnowSQL. The variable names will be set when you call SnowSQL. We have altered the variables names in this example so that you can see the difference from what was set in the config file.

1. Open a new terminal window and execute the following SnowSQL command. Note that this will work only if the connection variables are set. See "Connection Settings" to set up your config file.

    ```
    snowsql -D tablename=NATION -s TPCH_SF001
    -d SNOWFLAKE_SAMPLE_DATA
    ```

2. The SnowSQL application should open and be set to the database SNOWFLAKE_SAMPLE_DATA and the schema TPCH_SF001 (see Figure 5-6). Type the following commands:

```
!set variable_substitution=true
select count(*) from "&tablename";
```

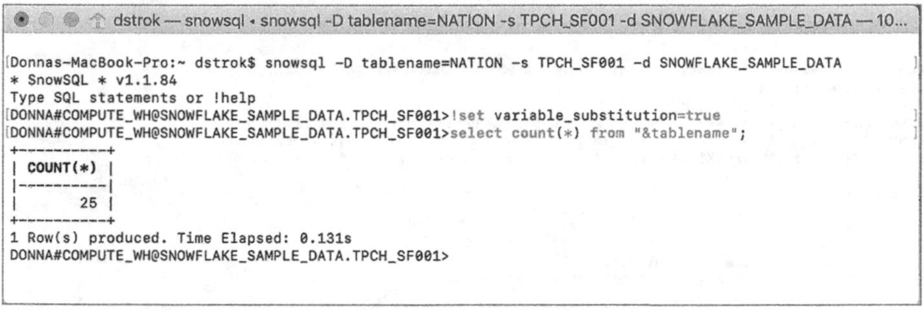

Figure 5-6. Setting variables while executing the SnowSQL command

Executing Variables in an Active Session

SnowSQL also lets you define variables while in an active session. The !define command must be used in order to set the variables. Walk through the following exercise to see how this is done:

1. Open a new terminal window and execute the following SnowSQL command. Note that this will work only if the connection variables are set. See "Connection Settings" to set up your config file. The database and schema name will be set during the connection.

```
snowsql -s TPCH_SF001 -d SNOWFLAKE_SAMPLE_DATA
```

2. SnowSQL will open; then enter the following
    SnowSQL commands. Your output should be similar
    to Figure 5-7.

    ```
    !define tablename=NATION
    !set variable_substitution=true
    select count(*) from "&tablename";
    ```

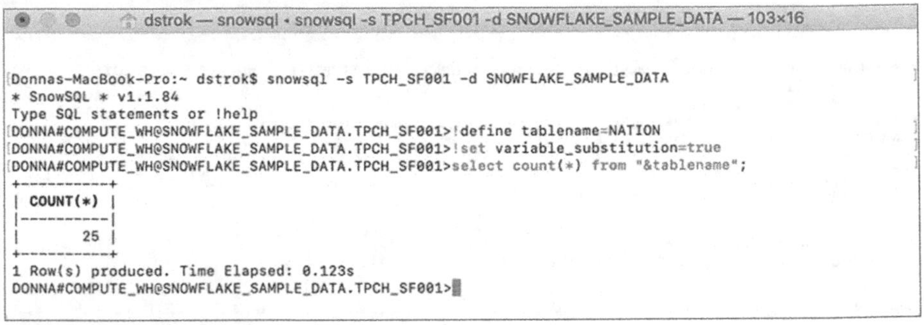

Figure 5-7. *Creating and using variables in an active SnowSQL session*

SnowSQL Commands

In a Snowflake session, you can issue commands to take specific actions.
All commands in SnowSQL start with an exclamation point, followed by
the command name. These commands can be listed by typing !help in
an active SnowSQL session. Table 5-1 displays the commands that can
help you through your automation process. You can also execute these
commands in an active SnowSQL session.

It is actually equivalent to a method with implementation of the switch conditional statement:

```
private static String convertDigit(int digit) {
        String s = "";
        switch(digit) {
                case 10:
                        s = "A";
                        break;
                case 11:
                        s = "B";
                        break;
                case 12:
                        s = "C";
                        break;
                case 13:
                        s = "D";
                        break;
                case 14:
                        s = "E";
                        break;
                case 15:
                        s = "F";
                        break;
                default:
                        s = Integer.toString(digit);
                        break;
        }
        return s;
}
```

Obviously, the approach using a string array is simpler.

Problems

1. Richa and Yashvi are going to Jamaica with their school. They plan on attending a fair where the admission for children is $1.50 and $4.00 for adults. On a specific day, 2,200 people enter the fair and $5,050 is collected. How many children attended? (2017 MathIsCool)

2. In a mathematics contest with 10 problems, a student gains 5 points for a correct answer and loses 2 points for an incorrect answer. If Olivia answered every problem and her score was 29, how many correct answers did she have? (2002 AMC8)

3. How many positive integers not exceeding 2001 are multiples of 3 or 4 but not 5? (2001 AMC10)

4. How many positive three-digit numbers contain exactly two distinct digits (e.g., 343 or 772, but not 589 or 111)? (2006 MathIsCool)

5. Rebecca goes to the store where she buys five plants. If the store sells three types of plants, how many different combinations of plants can she buy? (2005 MathIsCool)

Table 5-1. *SnowSQL Commands That Can Be Displayed by Using*
`!help` *in an Active Session*

Command	Description
`!abort`	Aborts a query. Use something like this: `!abort <query id>`
`!connect`	Creates a new connection. Use something like this: `!connect <connection_name>`
`!define`	Defines a variable as the given value. Use something like this: `!define <variable>=<value>`
`!edit`	Opens up a text editor. This is useful for writing longer queries. It defaults to the previous query. Use something like this: `!edit <query>`
`!exit (or !disconnect)`	Drops the current connection. Use something like this: `!disconnect`
`!help (or !helps, !h)`	Shows the client help. Use something like this: `!help`
`!options (or !opts)`	Shows all options and their values. Use something like this: `!options`
`!pause`	Pauses running queries. Use something like this: `!pause`

(continued)

Table 5-1. (*continued*)

Command	Description
!print	Prints given text; use something like this: !print <message>
!queries	Lists queries matching the specified filters. Use something like this: !queries help For a list of filters, add <filter>=<value>, <filter> to refine the command.
!quit (or !q)	Drops all connections and quits SnowSQL. Use something like this: !quit
!rehash	Refreshes autocompletion. Use something like this: !rehash
!result	Shows the result of a query. Use something like this: !result <query id> To find <query id>, see !queries.
!set	Sets an option to the given value. Use something like this: !set <option>=<value> See !options for all the options currently set.
!source (or !load)	Executes a given SQL file. Use something like this: !source <filename> You can use <url> in place of <filename>.

(continued)

Table 5-1. (*continued*)

Command	Description
!spool	Turns on or off writing the results to a file. Use something like this: !spool <filename> To turn it off, use this: !spool off
!system	Runs a system command in the shell. Use something like this: !system <system command>
!variables (or !vars)	Shows all variables and their values. Use something like this: !variables

Multiple Connection Names

SnowSQL supports multiple sessions (i.e., connections) with !connect <connection_name>. This can be especially useful if you have development, test, and production environments. The SnowSQL configuration file is where the different connections can be saved and split out by sections named as [connections.<connection_name>]. The default connection is always referenced by the [connections] section of the config file.

You can connect to more than one connection name at a time. When you open a connection, it will be added to a connection stack. Once your connection ends, then the previous connection will resume. If the quit command is used, then all connections in the stack will end.

CREATING SEPARATE ENVIRONMENT CONNECTIONS

For the purpose of this exercise, I will demonstrate how to connect to a development environment and then a production environment. There are a handful of ways to get this set up. I have seen separate Snowflake accounts or separate virtual warehouses in the same Snowflake account. However, I will show the latter, but note that you can simply swap out the value for `accountname` if you choose to open separate Snowflake accounts.

1. Open the config configuration file in a text editor. The default location of the file is as follows:

   Linux/macOS: ~/.snowsql/

   Windows: %USERPROFILE%\.snowsql\

2. Add the following text to the file, replace <your password> with your Snowflake account password, and save:

   ```
   [connections.development]
   password=<your password>
   warehousename=DEVELOPMENT

   [connections.production]
   password=<your password>
   warehousename=PRODUCTION
   ```

3. Open a terminal window and execute SNOWSQL to open a new SnowSQL session. Run the following CREATE WAREHOUSE statements. These two virtual warehouses are being created for demonstration purposes; therefore, the smallest virtual warehouse is being selected.

```
CREATE WAREHOUSE DEVELOPMENT WITH WAREHOUSE_SIZE =
'XSMALL' WAREHOUSE_TYPE = 'STANDARD' AUTO_SUSPEND = 600
AUTO_RESUME = TRUE MIN_CLUSTER_COUNT = 1 MAX_CLUSTER_
COUNT = 2 SCALING_POLICY = 'STANDARD';

CREATE WAREHOUSE PRODUCTION WITH WAREHOUSE_SIZE =
'XSMALL' WAREHOUSE_TYPE = 'STANDARD' AUTO_SUSPEND = 600
AUTO_RESUME = TRUE MIN_CLUSTER_COUNT = 1 MAX_CLUSTER_
COUNT = 2 SCALING_POLICY = 'STANDARD';
```

4. In the same terminal window, execute the following commands. The output should look similar to Figure 5-8.

```
!connect development
!connect production
!exit
!exit
!quit
```

```
● ● ●                ⌂ dstrok — -bash — 69×24
* SnowSQL * v1.1.84
Type SQL statements or !help
DONNA#COMPUTE_WH@(no database).(no schema)>!connect development
DONNA#DEVELOPMENT@(no database).(no schema)>!connect production
DONNA#PRODUCTION@(no database).(no schema)>!exit
DONNA#DEVELOPMENT@(no database).(no schema)>!exit
DONNA#COMPUTE_WH@(no database).(no schema)>!quit
Goodbye!
```

Figure 5-8. Connecting to development and production sessions in the same terminal window. !exit will exit the top connection in the stack, whereas !quit will exit all sessions at the same time and quit SnowSQL

Data Loading with SnowSQL

In this section, we will take the file named zips2000.csv and bulk load it into Snowflake using SnowSQL. This will demonstrate that bulk data loading using COPY can be scripted and be your path to data pipeline automation.

LOAD DATA USING SNOWSQL

1. Open a new terminal window and connect to your Snowflake account (see the preceding section in this chapter for detailed instructions on how to do this). Set the warehouse to COMPUTE_WH, the database to DEMO_DB, and the schema to PUBLIC.

   ```
   USE WAREHOUSE COMPUTE_WH;
   USE DATABASE DEMO_DB;
   USE SCHEMA PUBLIC;
   ```

2. Create a table named zipcodes2000_snowsql.

   ```
   CREATE OR REPLACE TABLE "ZIPCODES2000_SNOWSQL"
   ("ZIPCODE" STRING, "LON" DOUBLE, "LAT" DOUBLE);
   ```

3. Put the zips2000.csv file in the Snowflake staging area using the SnowSQL SFTP.

   ```
   put file:///Users/dstrok/documents/zips2000.csv
   @DEMO_DB.PUBLIC.%zipcodes2000_snowsql;
   ```

4. Copy the file contents into the Snowflake tables created in step 2.

   ```
   copy into zipcodes2000_snowsql
   from @%zipcodes2000_snowsql
   file_format = (type = csv field_optionally_enclosed_
   by='"' SKIP_HEADER = 1);
   ```

5.   Check the table to ensure that the data loaded.

```
select * from zipcodes2000_snowsql;
```

Summary

In this chapter, you learned how to install and configure SnowSQL. We also went over the SnowSQL commands. We demonstrated how to handle multiple Snowflake connections using SnowSQL. Last, we bulk loaded a CSV file into a Snowflake table using SnowSQL. You now have the tools to get your virtual warehouse set up with automation.

Continuous Data Loading with Snowpipe

"You and I are streaming data engines."

— Jeff Hawkins, in an interview by Knowstuff[1] from 2012

If you're a data analyst or data scientist or you're on an executive team, you know the value of access to continuous and timely data at any given time. You want to know that whenever you're querying data, transforming it, or accessing it in any way that the data represents the most up-to-date information available to use for data analysis.

If you have stale data, you might make inaccurate conclusions or have skewed statistics that will lead to misinformed strategic decisions that can affect your company down the line. Access to continuous data is a beneficial thing for anyone, regardless of role.

---

[1]https://www.knowstuff.org/2012/11/
 jeff-hawkins-develops-a-brainy-big-data-company/

© Dmitry Anoshin, Dmitry Shirokov, Donna Strok 2020
D. Anoshin et al., *Jumpstart Snowflake*, https://doi.org/10.1007/978-1-4842-5328-1_6

Nowadays, we know that data is generated much faster than it ever used to be before. In the past, corporate data would be updated infrequently, either daily or weekly or even monthly, and added to your data warehouse. Data accumulates over time, which leads to it becoming more and more challenging to process.

Now we have app data, mobile data, and data sensors that generate this constant flow of useful analytical data, but it can really be a challenge to get it into a data warehouse because it's being generated so quickly. Multitudes of tiny files are being generated, and that can definitely lead to problems.

Let's look at the traditional way of dealing with loading data into a data warehouse. Figure 6-1 shows data that's being generated continuously, loaded into a staging environment like S3, and then batched daily or hourly into your database.

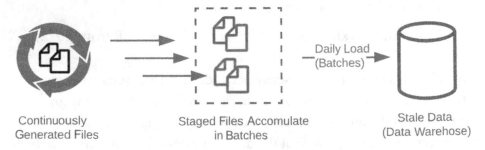

| Continuously | Staged Files Accomulate | Stale Data |
| Generated Files | in Batches | (Data Warehose) |

Figure 6-1. *Classical approach to loading into a data warehouse*

Unfortunately, this methodology allows for loading data only daily or hourly or even half-hourly. It does not provide fast access to the data that was generated. Users are often requesting the ability to analyze our data as quickly as it's coming in to make important decisions based on the results being generated.

If you decide to implement a continuously loading system, you're probably aware of is COPY command, which was designed for batch-loading scenarios. After accumulating data over some time, such as hours or days, you can then launch a COPY command to load data into your target table in Snowflake.

Note   The COPY command is mainly a SQL command for loading files into a Snowflake table. The command supports different options and file formats. Please see the Snowflake documentation.[2]

As a work around for near real-time task, you may leverage a micro-batching approach by using COPY command. It then takes a couple of minutes to use a COPY statement on a schedule to load it. However, it is still not a fully continuous load, because fresh data that arrives and ready for loading into data warehouse won't be triggered itself. Usually, humans or a scheduler drives it.

If you have data that's being generated continuously, you might think that it'd be great if there were an easily affordable, lightweight way to get your data up-to-date in Snowflake. Luckily, Snowflake agrees with you and created a service called Snowpipe. Snowpipe is an autoscaling Snowflake cloud service that provides continuously loaded data into the Snowflake data warehouse from internal and external stages.

With a continuous loading approach like Snowpipe, you have a data-driven way for new data to arrive from Snowflake to your target table.

Table 6-1 describes the data warehouse loading approaches.

---

[2]https://docs.snowflake.net/manuals/sql-reference/sql/copy-into-table.html

Table 6-1. *Data Warehouse Loading Approaches*

Approach	Definition	Snowpipe Options
Batch	Data accumulates over time (daily, hourly) and is then loaded periodically.	Point at an S3 bucket and a destination table in your warehouse where new data is automatically uploaded.
Microbatch	Data accumulates over small time windows (minutes) and then is loaded.	A technical resource can interface directly using a REST API[3] along with Java and Python SDKs to enable highly customized loading use cases.
Continuously (near real time)	Every data item is loaded individually as it arrives in near real time.	Also available is a way to integrate to Apache Kafka[4] using a Kafka connector.[5]

With Snowpipe you have two options. The first option is to use Snowpipe as a bucket AWS S3, where you define event notifications on your S3 bucket and then have these event notifications sent to Snowflake as soon as new files land in the S3 bucket. Those files are automatically picked up by Snowpipe and loaded into your target tables.

The second option is to build your own integration with Snowpipe using a REST API. You can create your own applications that will call the Snowpipe loader according to your criteria. In Table 6-2 you can find a summary of the critical benefits of using Snowpipe's service.

---

[3]For more information, see https://en.wikipedia.org/wiki/Representational_state_transfer.

[4]For more information, see https://kafka.apache.org/.

[5]For more information, see https://docs.snowflake.net/manuals/user-guide/kafka-connector.html.

Table 6-2. *Key Snowpipe Benefits*

Benefits	Description
Continuous loading, immediate insight.	Continuously generated data is available for analysis in seconds.
Avoid repeated manual COPY commands. High level of availability for building custom integration.	No manual effort is required for loading data into Snowflake. Automated loading with no need for manual COPY commands. Using a REST API and SDK, you can build your own data pipeline system.
Full support for semistructured data on load.	Availability of many industry-standard formats such as XML, JSON, Parquet, ORC, and Avro. No transformation is needed to load varying data types, and there's no trade-off between flexibility and performance.
You pay only for the compute time you use to load data.	The "pay only for what you use" pricing model means idle time is not charged for. Snowflake's built-for-the-cloud solution scales storage separately from compute, up and down, transparently, and automatically. This requires a full understanding of the cost of loading data. There is a separate expense item for "loading data" in your Snowflake bill. This has a serverless billing model via utilization-based billing.
Zero management.	No indexing, tuning, partitioning, or vacuuming on load.
Serverless.	Serverless loading without contention. No servers to manage and no impact to other workloads thanks to unlimited concurrency.

Loading Data Continuously

Let's take a closer look at some options for loading data.

- Snowpipe Auto-Ingest

- Snowpipe REST API using AWS Lambda

Snowpipe Auto-Ingest

Snowpipe Auto-Ingest is a fully automatic mode that loads data from the block store into the target table. The speed and ease of configuration provided by using DDL allows any data engineer or even analysts to configure their automatic continuous data loading process in minutes.

Caution   The option `auto_ingest` is not available unless it is explicitly enabled on your Snowflake account. Please contact Snowflake Support[6] for the enable options in your Snowflake account.

Figure 6-2 shows the main components of how this integration works. The data source provides continuous data feeds into services like AWS Kinesis,[7] AWS Managed Streaming for Kafka (MSK),[8] and Hosted Apache Kafka.[9] You can use them to stage your files into an external stage (e.g., S3 bucket) as soon as files arrive in the bucket. S3 sends

---

[6]E-mail: support@snowflake.com

[7]AWS Kinesis is group of services related to real-time and near-real-time data ingestion. For more information, see `https://aws.amazon.com/kinesis/`.

[8]For more about the AWS Managed Streaming service for Kafka, see `https://docs.aws.amazon.com/msk/latest/developerguide/what-is-msk.html`.

[9]Apache Kafka is an open source stream-processing software platform. For more information. see `https://kafka.apache.org/documentation/`.

a notification via an SQS queue[10] to Snowpipe, and as soon as that notification about a new file in the queue is received, Snowpipe runs a serverless loader application that loads the files from S3 into the target tables behind the scenes.

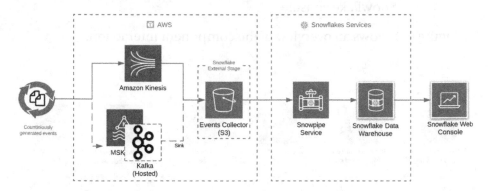

Figure 6-2. *Snowflake continuous data loading approach using Snowpipe with Auto-Ingest*

Building a Data Pipeline Using the Snowpipe Auto-Ingest Option

To build an example of a continuously loaded data pipeline, we need the following components:

- Stream Producer is a sample producer for Kinesis Data Firehose. For simplicity, in this case, instead of a stream producer based on the Lambda service, we just can use Firehose Test Generator, which is available to us when we are creating a Firehose stream.

- Kinesis Data Firehose as stream delivery service.

- S3 bucket as an external Snowflake stage.

---

[10]AWS SQS is an Amazon Queue service. For more information, see https:// docs.aws.amazon.com/sqs/index.html.

- The following Snowflake services:

    a. Snowpipe

    b. Snowflake data warehouse

    c. Snowflake console

Figure 6-3 shows an overview of the component interaction.

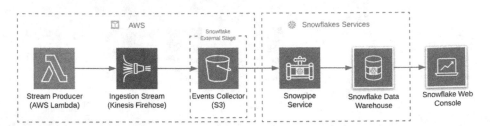

Figure 6-3. *Snowpipe data loading using Auto-Ingest mode*

To understand how internal integration actually takes place, we need to dive a little bit into the internal structure of Snowpipe. Figure 6-4 shows the main steps of integration.

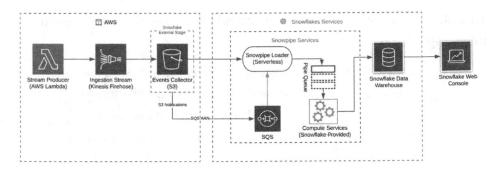

Figure 6-4. *Snowpipe data loading using Auto-Ingest mode, Snowpipe detail view*

First, we have to create an external *stage* and a *pipe* using the auto_ ingest option. When we execute the DDL, we have to get a unique identifier for an internal queue service (with AWS, it is based on SQS) that is already linked to the Snowpipe serverless loader.

Second, we must create a new S3 bucket and configure an S3 bucket event notification that has to send notification events into Snowpipe SNS. The Snowpipe loader gets events about the new file into an S3 bucket and queues pipe statements that contain specific COPY commands. Snowflake computes services fully and automatically scales when executing DDL statements from the pipe queue. The last step is to create and configure a stream that produces intensively a lot of events.

Caution   You cannot control transaction boundaries for load with Snowpipe.

> ### EXERCISE 1. BUILDING A DATA PIPELINE USING THE SNOWPIPE AUTO-INGEST OPTION

In this exercise, we will build the pipeline shown in Figure 6-3. Specifically, the following instructions show the process of creating a continuous data pipeline for Snowflake using Snowpipe:

1.   Log into your Snowflake account and choose Worksheet.

2.   Create Snowflake external stages based on an S3 bucket.

     Replace <your_AWS_KEY_ID> with your AWS credentials, and replace <your_s3_bucket> with your S3 bucket URL.

Run the DDL statements on the worksheet, as shown in Listing 6-1.

Listing 6-1. Creating External Stages

```
#create a new database for testing snowpipe
create database snowpipe data_retention_time_in_days = 1;
show databases like 'snow%';

# create a new external stage
create or replace stage snowpipe.public.snowstage
url='S3://<your_s3_bucket>'
credentials=(
AWS_KEY_ID='<your_AWS_KEY_ID>',
AWS_SECRET_KEY='<your_AWS_SEKRET_KEY>');

# create target table for Snowpipe
create or replace table snowpipe.public.snowtable(
    jsontext variant
);

# create a new pipe
create or replace pipe snowpipe.public.snowpipe
    auto_ingest=true as
            copy into snowpipe.public.snowtable
            from @snowpipe.public.snowstage
            file_format = (type = 'JSON');
```

Note   Variant is universal semistructured data type of Snowflake for loading data in formats such as JSON,[11] Avro,[12] ORC,[13] Parquet,[14] or XML.[15] For more information, you can refer to the references given.[16]

In the first part of Listing 6-1, we create a new external stage[17] called snowpipe.public.snowstage based on an S3 bucket, and we are providing the URL S3 bucket and the credentials.[18] Additionally, you can set encryption options.[19]

The next step is to define a target table called snowpipe.public. snowtable for the data that we want to load continuously. The table takes a variant column as input for the JSON data.

The last part of the script is a definition of a new pipe called snowpipe. public.snowpipe. You can see the pipe is set to auto_ingest=true, which means that we are using notifications from S3 into SQS to notify Snowflake about newly arrived data that is ready to load. Also, you can see that the pipe wraps a familiar COPY statement that defines the transformations and the data loading operations that we want to perform on the data as it becomes available.

---

[11]JSON file format: https://json.org/

[12]Apache AVRO file format: https://avro.apache.org/

[13]ORC file format: https://orc.apache.org/

[14]Parquet file format: https://parquet.apache.org/

[15]XML file format: https://en.wikipedia.org/wiki/XML

[16]For more information, see https://docs.snowflake.net/manuals/sql-reference/data-types-semistructured.html.

[17]For more information, see https://docs.snowflake.net/manuals/sql-reference/sql/create-stage.html.

[18]For more information, check https://docs.aws.amazon.com/general/latest/gr/aws-security-credentials.html.

[19]See https://docs.snowflake.net/manuals/sql-reference/sql/create-stage.html.

3. Check the correctness of the configuration using the following commands. Using show statements, you can see the status of any pipes and stages.

    ```
    # check exists pipes and stages
    show pipes;
    show stages;
    ```

4. Copy the SQS ARN link from the NotificationChannel field.

5. Using a simple select statement, we can check the count of loaded data.

    ```
    # check count of rows in target table
    select count(*) from snowpipe.public.snowtable
    ```

6. Log into your AWS account.

7. Create an AWS S3 bucket called snowpipebucket, as shown in Figure 6-5.

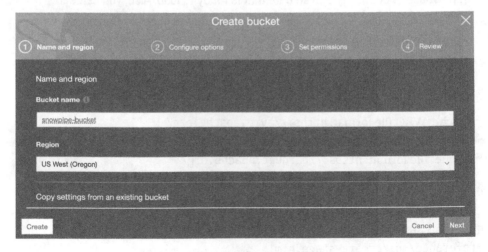

Figure 6-5. *Creating a new bucket for stream events*

8. Set notification events for S3 for Snowpipe using the path S3 ➤ snowpipebucket ➤ Properties ➤ Advanced settings ➤ Events, as shown in Figure 6-6.

Figure 6-6. *Setting S3 bucket notifications via SQS*

9. Create a new Kinesis Data Firehose stream using the path Amazon Kinesis ➤ Data Firehose ➤ Create Delivery Stream.

    You can see what that looks like in Figure 6-7.

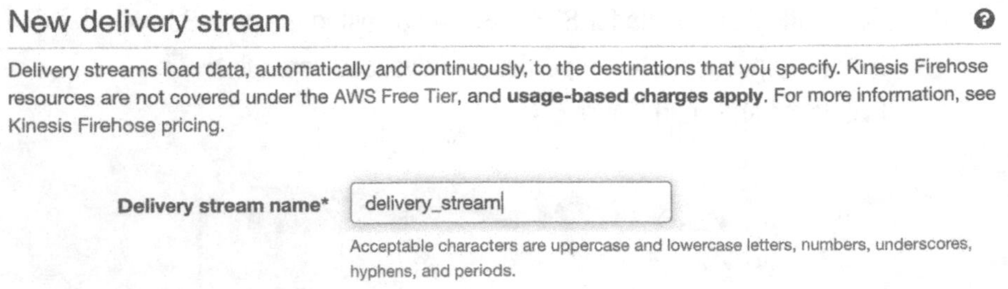

New delivery stream   ❓

Delivery streams load data, automatically and continuously, to the destinations that you specify. Kinesis Firehose
resources are not covered under the AWS Free Tier, and **usage-based charges apply**. For more information, see
Kinesis Firehose pricing.

Delivery stream name*   [delivery_stream|]

Acceptable characters are uppercase and lowercase letters, numbers, underscores,
hyphens, and periods.

Figure 6-7. *Creating a new Kinesis Firehose delivery stream*

10. Set the source to a direct PUT command, as shown in Figure 6-8.

Source*   ⊙ Direct PUT or other sources
Choose this option to send records directly to the delivery stream, or to send
records from AWS IoT, CloudWatch Logs, or CloudWatch Events.

Figure 6-8. *Set the type of source as a direct PUT statement*

11. Choose a destination for your S3 bucket, as shown in Figure 6-9.

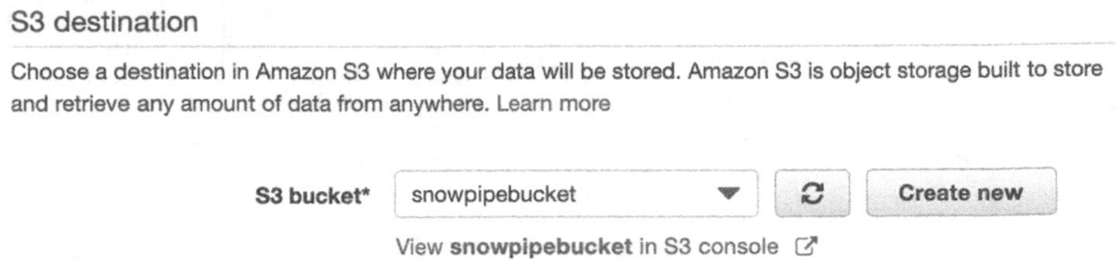

S3 destination

Choose a destination in Amazon S3 where your data will be stored. Amazon S3 is object storage built to store
and retrieve any amount of data from anywhere. Learn more

S3 bucket*   [snowpipebucket   ▼]   [⟳]   [**Create new**]

View **snowpipebucket** in S3 console ⧉

Figure 6-9. *Configuration of Firehose, setting up S3 bucket as destination*

12. Enable logging using the CloudWatch service, as shown in
Figure 6-10.

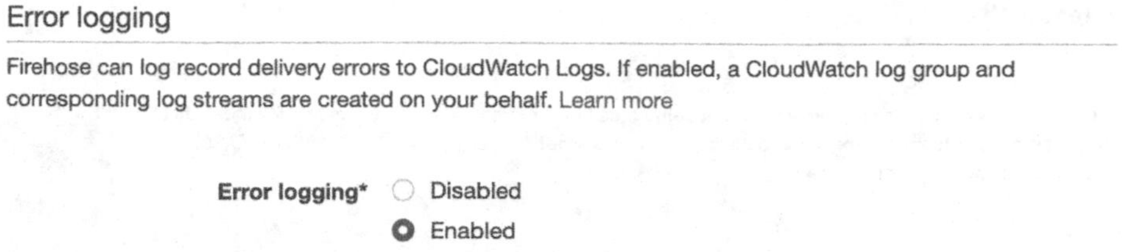

Error logging

Firehose can log record delivery errors to CloudWatch Logs. If enabled, a CloudWatch log group and corresponding log streams are created on your behalf. Learn more

Error logging*   ○ Disabled
                      ● Enabled

Figure 6-10. *Enabling CloudWatch logging*

13. Create an IAM role with a policy, as follows:

    . . .

```
        {
            "Sid": "",
            "Effect": "Allow",
            "Action": [
                "s3:AbortMultipartUpload",
                "s3:GetBucketLocation",
                "s3:GetObject",
                "s3:ListBucket",
                "s3:ListBucketMultipartUploads",
                "s3:PutObject"
            ],
            "Resource": [
                "arn:aws:s3:::snowpipebucket",
                "arn:aws:s3:::snowpipebucket/*",
            ]
        },
```
    . . .

14. Run the testing stream, as shown in Figure 6-11.

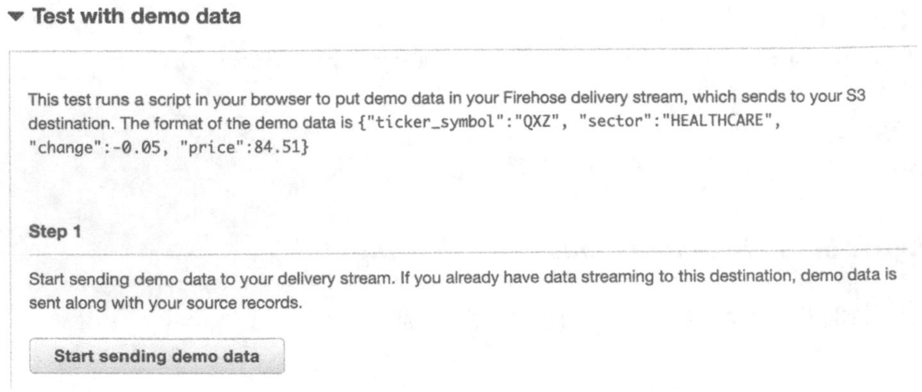

▼ **Test with demo data**

This test runs a script in your browser to put demo data in your Firehose delivery stream, which sends to your S3 destination. The format of the demo data is {"ticker_symbol":"QXZ", "sector":"HEALTHCARE", "change":-0.05, "price":84.51}

Step 1

Start sending demo data to your delivery stream. If you already have data streaming to this destination, demo data is sent along with your source records.

    Start sending demo data

Figure 6-11. *Testing*

15. Check the file in the S3 bucket.

16. Check the count of loaded data.

```
# check count of rows in target table
select count(*) from snowpipe.public.snowtable
```

Snowpipe REST API Using AWS Lambda

If the Auto-Ingest option is not available to your account for some reason, you will need a flexible way to integrate with other services so that you can still implement your code through the Snowpipe REST API.

Figure 6-12 shows how to build a pipeline with a custom app using the REST API.

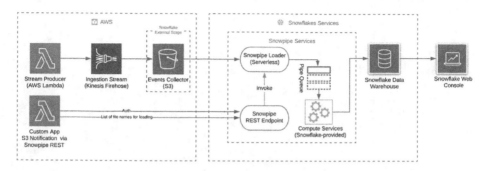

Figure 6-12. *Snowpipe data loading using Auto-Ingest mode*

Figure 6-12 shows the second option. On the left side, you can see your application. This can be an actual application if you are running one on a virtual machine or a Docker container, but it also can be code that you are running on AWS Lambda. Your Lambda function or application then takes care of placing the load files in the S3 bucket as soon as the file is persisted there.

Snowpipe then adds these files to a queue behind the REST API endpoint. You will invoke the REST API, and that will invoke the Snowpipe loader service, which works off of that queue to load the data into the target tables that you have defined. For step-by-step instructions to do this, you can refer to the official documentation.[20]

Summary

In this chapter, we covered Snowpipe features that allow you to continuously build a data pipeline. In addition, you learned about billing and considered several basic options for using the features. Finally, you built data pipelines based on Snowpipe integrations.

In the next chapter, we will discuss Snowflake administration and cover the primary Snowflake objects in more detail.

---

[20]https://docs.snowflake.net/manuals/user-guide/data-load-snowpipe-rest-lambda.html

CHAPTER 7

Snowflake Administration

Snowflake is a database, and as such it comes with similar administration features as any other database. It was also the first data warehouse as a service (DWaaS), meaning that end users can do a minimum of administration and maintenance.

This chapter provides an overview of options for managing your Snowflake account, geared primarily to Snowflake administrators. However, it is also useful for end users to understand the key concepts of Snowflake administration and management.

There are several main tasks required of administrators:

- Administering roles and users

- Administering account parameters

- Administering resource consumption

- Administering databases and warehouses

- Administering data shares

- Administering database objects

- Administering clustered tables

We will cover all these topics and show how it works using our Snowflake demo.

© Dmitry Anoshin, Dmitry Shirokov, Donna Strok 2020
D. Anoshin et al., *Jumpstart Snowflake*, https://doi.org/10.1007/978-1-4842-5328-1_7

Administering Roles and Users

Snowflake uses *roles* for managing access and operations. In other words, you can create custom roles with a set of privileges to control the granularity of the access granted. For instance, say we want to create a role for our marketing team, which will grant the team members access to the data and allow them to run SQL queries using a virtual warehouse. According to the Snowflake model, access to securable objects is managed by *privileges* assigned to roles. Moreover, roles can be assigned to other roles and users.

Snowflake leverages the following access control models:

- **Discretionary access control (DAC)**: Each object has an owner, and this owner can manage the access of the object.

- **Role-based access control (RBAC)**: Roles are created and assigned privileges, and then the roles are assigned to users.

Note   A *securable object* is a Snowflake entity to which access can be granted (i.e., database, table, access, and so on). A *privilege* is a level of access to an object.

Figure 7-1 shows an example of the Marketing role that grants the privileges USAGE, MODIFY, and OPERATE to the securable objects DATABASE and WAREHOUSE for marketing users.

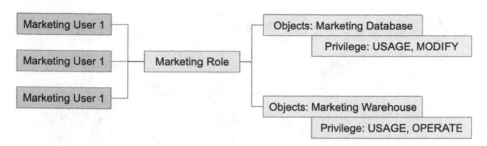

Figure 7-1. *Example of Marketing role that is granted specific privileges for marketing users*

When we launched our example Snowflake account, it had a number of predefined default roles.

- **ACCOUNTADMIN**: This account administrator role is the top-level role for a Snowflake account.

- **SYSADMIN**: This system administrator role is for creating and managing databases and warehouse.

- **PUBLIC**: This is a pseudo-role that can be assigned to any object, but they all will be available for all account users.

- **SECURITYADMIN**: This security administrator role is for creating and managing roles and users.

You can create custom roles with the SECURITYADMIN role, or you can grant the CREATE ROLE privilege to any new role. For any custom role, you should think about the role hierarchy in order to assign your new custom role to the one of the high-level administration roles. Figure 7-2 shows an example of this hierarchy. It shows the Marketing role, which has privileges for the marketing database, schema, and warehouse that belong to the SYSADMIN role.

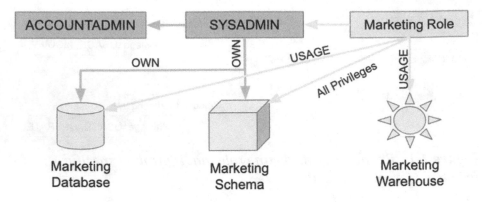

Figure 7-2. *This is an example of a custom role hierarchy*

Enforcement Model

When you are connecting your Snowflake account with the web interface or ODBC/JDBC, a session is initiated, and it has a current role that consists of managed permissions for user. It is possible to change the role using the USE ROLE command or to switch roles by using the menu in the top-right corner.

Figure 7-3. *Role switching*

When a user wants to perform any action in Snowflake, Snowflake will compare the user's role privileges against the required privileges.

Note   You may be familiar with the concept of a super-user or super-role with other database vendors, but you will not find this functionality in Snowflake. All access requires the appropriate access privileges.

Working with Roles and Users

Snowflake allows you to control your data warehouse at a granular level within roles. To create a role, you can execute DDL commands or use the web interface. The following commands are available:

- CREATE ROLE: Creates a new role

- ALTER ROLE: Changes an existing role

- DROP ROLE: Drops an existing role

- SHOW ROLES: Shows a list of available roles

- USE ROLE: Switches a role for the session

Let's create a new role. Log into your Snowflake account and make sure that you choose the SECURITYADMIN role.

```
CREATE ROLE MARKETING_TEAM;
```

This command will create a role. Next, grant permissions for this role and attach users. The following commands are available for user management:

- CREATE USER: Creates a new user

- ALTER USER: Changes an existing user

- DESCRIBE USER: Describes an existing user

- SHOW PARAMETERS: Shows the parameters of the user

In addition, we can specify the following options for users:

- userProperties: Properties such as password, display name, and so on.

- sessionParams: Session options such as default warehouse and namespace

Let's run a command that will create a new user and assign him to the MARKETING_TEAM role.

```
CREATE USER marketing_analyst PASSWORD = 'RockYourData' COMMENT
= 'Marketing Analyst' LOGIN_NAME = 'marketing_user1' DISPLAY_
NAME = 'Marketing_Analyst' DEFAULT_ROLE = "MARKETING_TEAM"
DEFAULT_WAREHOUSE = 'SF_TUTS_WH' MUST_CHANGE_PASSWORD = TRUE;
GRANT ROLE "MARKETING_TEAM" TO USER marketing_analyst;
```

You can achieve the same result using the web interface.

The last part of the code grants privileges for the MARKETING_TEAM role so new users can run SQL queries. We should grant OPERATE and USAGE for the virtual warehouse to our new role, like this:

```
GRANT USAGE ON WAREHOUSE SF_TUTS_WH TO ROLE MARKETING_TEAM;
GRANT OPERATE ON WAREHOUSE SF_TUTS_WH TO ROLE MARKETING_TEAM;
```

Note   SF_TUTS_WH is a small virtual warehouse that was created previously, but you can use your own warehouse. For demo purposes, it is always good to use the smallest computing instance.

Again, we can use the web interface to perform the same actions. Then we can log in with a new user, using login marketing_user1, and run this sample query:

```
SELECT * FROM "SNOWFLAKE_SAMPLE_DATA"."TPCH_SF1"."REGION"
```

If you want to achieve the same result using the web interface, you should navigate to the Account menu, as shown in Figure 7-4.

Figure 7-4. Account menu

By default the Account menu is available for the role ACCOUNTADMIN. This menu is usually accessible for Snowflake administrators. It allows them to manage users and roles, control credit usage, and so on.

Administering Resource Consumption

The next important topic for Snowflake administrators is resource consumption. Keeping track of storage and compute resources is critical for Snowflake customers. Snowflake provides administrative capabilities for monitoring credit and storage usage as well as provides resource monitors that can send alerts on usage spikes and automatically suspend the virtual warehouse.

By default, only the ACCOUNTADMIN role has access to the billing information. But this access can be provided for other users and roles with the monitor usage permissions.

As you know, Snowflake has a unique architecture that splits compute resources (virtual warehouses) and data storage. The cost of Snowflake consists of these two elements and is based on credits. In our case, when we created the Snowflake demo account for this book, we were granted 400 credits, and we are tracking consumption.

Virtual Warehouse Usage

You are already familiar with virtual warehouses (VWs) and its T-shirt sizes. Snowflake will charge credits for using a VW. In other words, the price depends on the number of VWs, their size, and how long they are running queries.

Note   Credits are billed per second, with a 60-second minimum.

You can use the table function WAREHOUSE_METERING_HISTORY that will show us hourly credit usage, or you can use web interface and click Account ➤ Billing & Usage. Let's run this code to see the usage for the last seven days:

```
select * from table(information_schema.warehouse_metering_
history(dateadd('days',-7,current_date())));
```

In addition, we can specify the VW name as a parameter. Figure 7-5 shows an example of sample usage.

Running Time	Credits (X-Small)	Credits (X-Large)	Credits (3X-Large)
0-60 seconds	0.018	0.264	1.068
61 seconds	0.018	0.268	1.086
2 minutes	0.036	0.528	2.136
10 minutes	0.18	2.64	10.68
1 hour	1	16	64

Figure 7-5. *Sample usage of credits for virtual warehouse for the XS, XL, and 3XL instance sizes*

Data Storage Usage

Another aspect of the price is storage. Snowflake calculates the price of storage monthly based on the average daily storage space. It includes files stored in the Snowflake stage, data stored in databases, and historical data maintained for a fail-safe. Moreover, time traveling and cloned objects are consuming storage. The price is based on a flat rate per terabyte (TB).

Note   The TB price depends on the type of account (capacity or on-demand), region, and cloud provider.

We can review the usage data using the web interface, as shown in Figure 7-6.

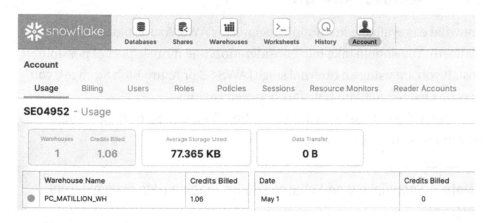

Figure 7-6. *Snowflake usage report*

Also, you can leverage table functions and a Snowflake view, as shown here:

```
#Database Storage for last 7 days
select * from table(information_schema.database_storage_usage_
history(dateadd('days',-7,current_date()),current_date()));
```

```
#Stage Storage for last 7 days
select * from table(information_schema.stage_storage_usage_
history(dateadd('days',-7,current_date()),current_date()));
```

```
#Table Storage utilization
select * from table_storage_metrics
```

Note   Make sure that data is in a compressed format in the
Snowflake staging area. Another consideration is to use external
storage options like Amazon S3 where you can set the data lifecycle
policy and archive cold data.

Data Transfer Usage

Snowflake is available in multiple regions for AWS, Azure, Google Cloud
Platform. You should take into consideration one more aspect of possible
cost. If you are using an external stage (AWS S3 or Azure Blob Storage), you
may be charged for data transfers between regions.

Snowflake charges a fee for unloading data into S3 or Blog Storage
within the same region or across regions.

Note   Snowflake won't charge you for loading data from external
storage.

There is an internal Snowflake function that will help us to track this
cost, as shown here:

```
#Cost for the last 7 days
select * from table(information_schema.data_transfer_
history(date_range_start=>dateadd('day',-7,current_
date()),date_range_end=>current_date()));
```

Administering Databases and Warehouses

There are a number of actions we can do with databases and warehouses. As usual, you have a choice to use the web interface or execute SQL commands.

We covered VWs in Chapter 2. In this section, we will review actions that we can do with VWs and databases.

Managing Warehouses

As an administrator, you can use the following commands with warehouses:

- CREATE WAREHOUSE

- DROP WAREHOUSE

- ALTER WAREHOUSE

- USE WAREHOUSE

When you are creating a new warehouse, you are specifying parameters such as size, type, and so on. Let's create a new warehouse by executing this command:

```
CREATE WAREHOUSE RYD WITH WAREHOUSE_SIZE = 'XSMALL' WAREHOUSE_
TYPE = 'STANDARD' AUTO_SUSPEND = 300 AUTO_RESUME = TRUE COMMENT
= 'Rock Your Data Virtual Warehouse';
```

We chose the smallest possible warehouse size, XSMALL. In addition, we have two additional parameters.

- AUTO SUSPEND: This will stop the warehouse if it is idle for more than 300 seconds.

- AUTO RESUME: This will start a suspended warehouse when needed.

You also have an option to resize the warehouse using the ALTER WAREHOUSE command. Finally, you can use the command USE WAREHOUSE to specify which warehouse to use for the current session.

Note   ALTER WAREHOUSE is a unique feature. It exists only in Snowflake. This command suspends or resumes a virtual warehouse or aborts all queries (and other SQL statements) for a warehouse. It can also be used to rename or set/unset the properties for a warehouse. There are more details available at https://docs. snowflake.net/manuals/sql-reference/sql/alter- warehouse.html.

Managing Databases

All data in Snowflake is stored in database tables. It is structured as a collection of columns and rows. For each database, we can define one or many schemas. Inside each schema, we are creating database objects such as tables and views.

Note   Snowflake doesn't have a hard limit on the number of databases, schemas, or database objects.

These are the commands available for database management:

- CREATE DATABASE
- CREATE DATABASE CLONE
- ALTER DATABASE
- DROP DATABASE

- UNDROP DATABASE

- USE DATABASE

- SHOW DATABASES

These commands could be executed via the web interface of SQL. Let's create a database.

```
CREATE DATABASE MARKETING_SANDBOX;
```

In addition, we can grant privileges such as CREATE SCHEMA, MODIFY, MONITOR, and USAGE for a specific role.

Overall, the operations look similar to traditional databases. However, there are a couple of unique features that are worth mentioning.

First is UNDROP DATABASE. Let's imagine that you accidentally drop the production database. Restoring it from backup could take at least a day. But not with Snowflake, where you can instantly restore the most recent version of a dropped database if you are within the defined retention window for that database.

Zero-Copy Cloning

Another unique feature is *zero-copy cloning*, which creates a snapshot of a database. This snapshot is writable and independent. These types of features are like a "dream come true" for data warehouse DBAs.

There are many situations where people need to copy their database to test or experiment with their data to avoid altering their sensitive production database. However, copying data can be painful and time-consuming because all the data needs to be physically moved from the production database to the database copy. This is extremely expensive because both copies of the data need to be paid for. When a production database gets updates, the database copy becomes stale and requires an update.

Snowflake takes a different approach. It enables us to test and experiment with our data more freely. It allows us to copy databases in seconds. Snowflake doesn't physically copy data. It continues to reference the original data and will store new records only when you update or change the data; therefore, you will pay for each unique record only once. Finally, we can use zero-copy cloning with the Time Travel feature.

Figure 7-7 shows an option for cloning a database using the web interface.

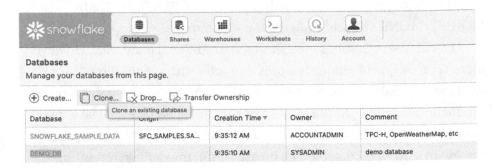

Figure 7-7. *Web interface for cloning a database*

As usual, we have the option to execute a command. Here are examples of commands with definitions:

```
--Clone a database and all objects within the database at its
current state:
create database mytestdb_clone clone mytestdb;
--Clone a schema and all objects within the schema at its
current state:
create schema mytestschema_clone clone testschema;
--Clone a table at its current state:
create table orders_clone clone orders;
--Clone a schema as it existed before the date and time in the
specified timestamp:
```

```
create schema mytestschema_clone_restore clone testschema
before (timestamp => to_timestamp(40*365*86400));
--Clone a table as it existed exactly at the date and time of
the specified timestamp:
create table orders_clone_restore clone orders at (timestamp
=> to_timestamp_tz('04/05/2013 01:02:03', 'mm/dd/yyyy
hh24:mi:ss'));
```

Administering Account Parameters

Parameters control the behavior of our Snowflake account, individual user sessions, and objects. All parameters are available on the Snowflake documentation page.

We can split all the parameters into types:

- **Account parameters:** These are set at the account level.

- **Sessions parameters (majority):** These are set for the session, user, and account.

- **Object parameters:** These are set for the account and object.

To override the default parameters, you can use the following commands:

- `ALTER ACCOUNT`

- `ALTER SESSION`

- `CREATE <object>` or `ALTER <object>`

To see the available parameters and their options, run the following:

```
show parameters;
```

Moreover, we can look the parameters for a specific database or warehouse.

These are some examples of parameters:

- STATEMENT_TIMEOUT_IN_SECONDS: Specifies the amount of time after which a running SQL statement is canceled by the system. This parameter will help to control end users and prevent bad and heavy queries.

- MAX_CONCURRENCY_LEVEL: Specifies the maximum number of SQL statements a warehouse cluster can execute concurrently.

- TIMEZONE: Specifies the time zone setting for the session.

Administering Database Objects

One of the most common administration tasks within Snowflake is to manage database objects such as tables, views, schemas, stages, file formats, and so on.

All database objects are created under the schema. Traditional databases objects such as table, view, materialized view, and sequence have similar options:

- CREATE

- ALTER

- DROP

- SHOW

- DESCRIBE

Moreover, Snowflake Administartor may leverage Snowflake unique capabilities like UNDROP and zero-copy cloning.

Another set of schema-level objects that are used in Snowflake include the following:

- **Stage**: Used for storing data files; could be internal and external

- **File format**: File format options (CSV, Parquet, etc.) and formatting options for each file type

- **Pipe**: Single copy statement for loading a set of data files

- **UDF**: User-defined function; a custom function that consists of SQL and JavaScript

As a Snowflake administrator, you may need to manage these objects.

Administering Data Shares

Secure data shares are another unique feature of Snowflake and will be covered in Chapter 10. This feature allows you to become a data provider by creating a data share using the CREATE SHARE command. By default, this is available only for the ACCOUNTADMIN role.

These are the available commands:

- CREATE SHARE

- ALTER SHARE

- DROP SHARE

- DESCRIBE SHARE

- SHOW SHARE

Note   As a share creator, you are responsible for data security. Before you create a share, you should spend some time to learn more about data and use cases to prevent the sharing of sensitive data. Secure views and UDFs are handy to use when creating shares.

After share creation, an admin can view, grant, or revoke access to database objects using the following commands:

- `GRANT <privilege> TO SHARE`: Grants access to share

- `REVOKE <privilege> TO SHARE`: Revokes access to share

- `SHOW GRANTS TO SHARE`: Shows all object privileges that have been granted to share

- `SHOW GRANTS OF SHARE`: Shows all accounts for the share and accounts that are using shares

In some cases, if you don't need to share anymore and want to drop it, you should consider the downstream impact for all consumers. As an option, you may revoke grants on some objects and see the result.

Administering Clustered Tables

As you know, Snowflake is a data warehouse as a service. The idea here is simple: you just use the data warehouse, and you don't need to think about data distribution, sorting, and table statistics.

One aspect of Snowflake performance is micro-partitioning. When we are loading data into Snowflake, it is automatically divided into micro-partitions with 50 MB to 500 MB of compressed data. These micro-partitions are organized in a columnar fashion. In addition, Snowflake collects and stores metadata in micro-partitions. This helps to optimize query plans and improve query performance by avoiding unnecessary scanning of micro-partitions through an operation known as *partition pruning*.

Snowflake also stores data in tables and tries to sort it along natural dimensions such as date and/or geographic regions. This is called *data clustering*, and it is a key factor for query performance. It is important, especially for large tables. By default, Snowflake uses automatic clustering. However, in some cases we may define the clustering key within the CREATE TABLE statement to change the default behavior. This should be an exception rather than a rule. In most cases, admins will not need to cluster. Best practice is to avoid clustering unless there is a specific query pattern that does not meet the SLA. In general, you should not need to cluster unless the table is at least 1 TB.

As a Snowflake administrator, you may need to review table clustering and run reclustering processes to identify all the problem tables and provide the best possible performance.

There are two system functions that allow us to monitor clustering information for tables:

- SYSTEM$CLUSTERING_DEPTH: This calculates the average depth of the table according to the specific columns.

- SYSTEM$CLUSTERING_INFORMATION: This calculates clustering details, including clustering depth, for a specific table.

If you need to improve the clustering of data, you should create a new table with a new clustering key and insert data into the new table, or you can use materialized views (MVs) to create a version of the table with the new cluster key. Then the MV function will automatically keep the MV data in sync with the new data added to the base table.

Note   A table with clustering keys defined is considered to be clustered. Clustering keys aren't important for all tables. Whether to use clustering depends on the size of a table and the query performance, and it is most suitable for multiterabyte tables.

Snowflake Materialized Views

When working with Teradata, we worked with materialized views (MVs) a lot. Basically, we had a complex SQL query that could produce metrics and dimensions for a business intelligence solution. Because of complex SQL logic, joins, and derived columns, we used MVs for improving query performance. However, traditional MVs had their downsides. For example, it was important to keep data in the VM up-to-date and refresh it daily with an ETL process. In addition, we experienced slowdowns in performance while updating the MVs using Data Manipulation Language commands.

Snowflake engineers didn't abandon the MV concept and added this functionality to Enterprise Edition. According to Snowflake, a *materialized view* is a precomputed data set derived from a query specification (the SELECT in the view definition) and stored for later use. Because the data is precomputed, querying a materialized view is faster than executing the original query. This performance difference can be significant when a query is run frequently or is sufficiently complex.

Note   Materialized views are designed to improve query performance for workloads composed of common, repeated query patterns. However, materializing intermediate results incurs additional costs. As such, before creating any materialized views, you should consider whether the costs are offset by the savings from reusing these results frequently.

There are a couple use cases when we can benefit from using MVs:

- The query results contain a small number of rows and/or columns relative to the base table (the table on which the view is defined).

- The query results require significant processing, including the following:

  - Analysis of semistructured data

  - Aggregates that take a long time to calculate

The main benefit of Snowflake MVs is that they solve the issues of traditional MVs. MVs are views that are automatically maintained by Snowflake. There is a background service that updates the materialized view after changes are made to the base table. This is more efficient and less error-prone than manually maintaining the equivalent of a materialized view at the application level.

Table 7-1 shows the key similarities and differences between tables, regular views, cached query results, and materialized views.

Table 7-1. *Key Similarities and Differences*

	Performance Benefits	Security Benefits	Simplifies Query Logic	Supports Clustering	Uses Storage	Uses Credits for Maintenance
Regular table				👍	👍	
Regular view		👍	👍			
Cached query result	👍					
Materialized view	👍	👍	👍	👍	👍	👍

Summary

In this chapter, we covered the main Snowflake administrative duties (e.g., user and role administration), and you learned about key Snowflake objects (e.g., warehouses and schema-level objects). In addition, we reviewed billing and usage information. Finally, we covered data shares and data clustering concepts as well as materialized views.

In the next chapter, you will learn about one of the key elements of cloud analytics: security.

CHAPTER 8

Snowflake Security Overview

For many organizations, it is challenging to be able to provide security today, especially in the cloud, given the number of threats and attacks that are occurring daily. Safeguarding data is paramount for Snowflake. The Snowflake services platform was built with security in mind from the beginning. The company has implemented a security framework that we believe addresses a lot of their customers' compliance challenges today.

Security is an important aspect in today's world. Developers have to secure their data and prevent unauthorized access to it, which is why Snowflake encrypts all the data automatically, including data at rest and in transit. In addition, Snowflake provides multifactor authentication and performs federated authentication.

One of the challenges with on-premises solutions is that data can reside at many different locations, so controlling the data flow and who's accessing it is challenging. With the cloud, you can build the right security controls to safeguard your data, but security doesn't stop there. There are many more aspects that are related to monitoring and ensuring the system is constantly protected.

The Snowflake platform is a cloud-native solution, and it provides security so that you don't need to worry; in other words, it is managed for you. Snowflake provides an end-to-end security solution to its customers, from when the data leaves a customer's premises through the untrusted

© Dmitry Anoshin, Dmitry Shirokov, Donna Strok 2020
D. Anoshin et al., *Jumpstart Snowflake*, https://doi.org/10.1007/978-1-4842-5328-1_8

Internet to the point when it arrives at the Snowflake storage; all along the way, the data is protected. Moreover, Snowflake hardens all the virtual machines that data resides on. Snowflake encrypts data, does audits, monitors, sends alerts, and installs patches on a continuous basis. All of this actually simplifies and facilitates the security efforts of customers. So, the customer does not necessarily have to incur all the procedural and compliance costs associated with security.

In this chapter, you will learn about the main Snowflake security features:

- Snowflake security reference architecture

- Network and site access

- Account and user authentication

- Object security

- Data security

- Security validations

Snowflake Security Reference Architecture

As you might know from previous chapters, Snowflake has a multicluster shared data architecture. It separates the process of working with data and information into three distinct layers.

- Storage layer, where all the data is stored in a columnar compressed format and is always encrypted.

- Compute layer, comprised of virtual warehouses, which are the compute nodes that perform all of the data processing. Multiple virtual warehouses can work on the same data at the same time.

- Services layer, also known as the "brains" of Snowflake.
  This is where all security information/metadata
  is stored and also where all query processing is
  completed. The service layer also includes transaction
  management, which coordinates across all of the
  virtual warehouses, allowing for a consistent set of
  operations against the same data at the same time.

This unique architecture allows Snowflake to ensure a high standard of security for its customers. Figure 8-1 shows Snowflake's security reference architecture. It describes the components that make up Snowflake's secure data warehouse. We will cover the key elements of this diagram in this chapter.

Note   This chapter will cover the security features that are available to date. Snowflake is constantly working on adding new features.

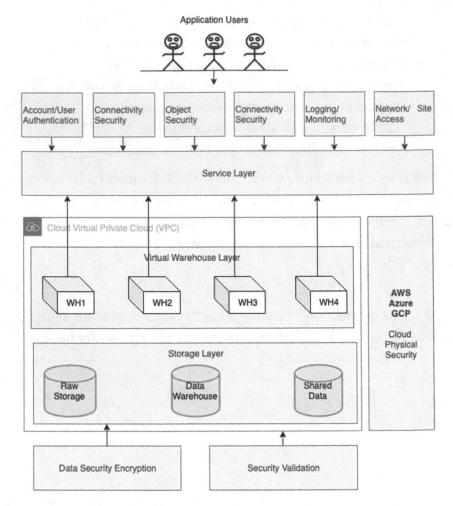

Figure 8-1. *Snowflake security reference architecture*

Virtual Private Cloud

First is the concept of a *virtual private cloud* (VPC). Snowflake is implemented as a VPC within the cloud provider's infrastructure. If a customer requires complete isolation from other Snowflake customers because of strict security requirements such as in the case of a financial institution, the Virtual Private Snowflake (VPS) edition must be used. When implemented, VPS is a Snowflake implementation entirely on its own VPC within the cloud provider's infrastructure.

Physical Security

Each cloud provider, including Amazon Web Services, Microsoft Azure, and Google Cloud Platform, provide their own infrastructure and physical security to guard all of their cloud data. Physical security includes 24-hour armed guards and video surveillance to ensure no unauthorized access is allowed in the data center. Neither Snowflake personnel nor Snowflake customers have access to these data centers. Data redundancy is also a standard practice implemented by the cloud provider for data recovery.

You can learn more about physical security from each cloud vendor by visiting their documentation.

Network and Site Access

All customer access to the Snowflake service via the Internet is made via the secure protocol HTTPS. Moreover, all Internet communications between users and the Snowflakes service are secured and encrypted using TLS1.2 or higher.

All communication between connection methods and Snowflake is secure, regardless of the method used to connect, whether via the web user interface or ODBC or JDBC connectors. Authentication is required to gain access to Snowflake. These connections are encrypted and communicate solely over HTTPS.

Access to Snowflake is subject to network policies. These policies provide options for managing network configurations to the Snowflake service, such as restricting access to an account based on a user IP address. Currently, Snowflake customers can implement a network policy to create an IP *whitelist*, which is a list of allowed IP addresses, as well as an IP *blacklist*, which lists those IP addresses that are forbidden access.

Figure 8-2 shows the Snowflake web UI for managing access policies.

Moreover, you can manage policies using SQL commands. Usually, we will specify the IP address of our organization and will give access to Snowflake only to our employees. We don't want to have a publicly available Snowflake endpoint.

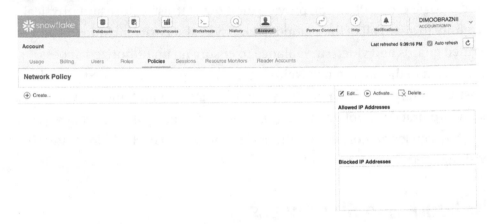

Figure 8-2. *Managing access policies*

For increased network connectivity security, private and direct communication between Snowflake and other VPCs can be set up via an AWS private link (in the case of AWS deployment). This feature, which effectively creates a private tunnel of communication between Snowflake and the VPC, is currently available only for the Business Critical Edition, formerly known as Enterprise for Sensitive Data (ESD), or VPS customers.

Account and User Authentication

For account access and user authentication, multifactor authentication (MFA) can be implemented for increased security on account access by users. MFA support is provided as an integrated Snowflake feature powered by the Duo security service and managed completely by Snowflake.

The only additional task after enabling MFA is to install the Duo mobile application, which is supported on multiple smartphone platforms including iOS, Android, and Windows.

Currently, each user must enable MFA by themselves. As a security best practice, all users with the account admin role should enroll with MFA.

Single sign-on (SSO) is a user authentication method that, once enabled, allows users to authenticate through an external SAML 2.0–compliant identity provider known as an IDP.

When authenticated, users can securely initiate one or more sessions in Snowflake for the duration of their IDP session. These sessions can be initiated from within the interface provided by the IDP or directly from within Snowflake. This feature is available for customers on Enterprise Edition and up.

Object Security

Access to specific objects within Snowflake, such as warehouses, databases, schemas, tables, etc., is controlled by a hybrid model of discretionary access control (DAC) and role-based access control (RBACK).

Note   *Discretionary access control* (DAC) is when each object has an owner, who can in turn grant access to that object. *Role-based access control* (RBAC) is when access privileges are assigned to roles, which are in turn assigned to users.

Discretionary access control means that each object created has an owner and that owner has control over the object. Role-based access control, as shown in Figure 8-3, makes use of roles that can be granted access to objects. These roles, in turn, can be granted to other roles or directly to users. The security admin system role in Snowflake is responsible for managing these privileges.

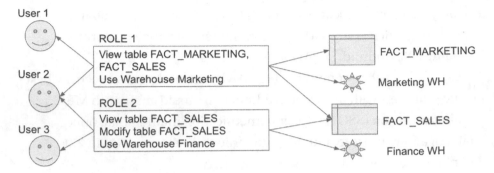

Figure 8-3. *Role-based access control*

Data Security

Encryption is enabled by default in Snowflake. All customer data is encrypted at rest. This includes not only the database data but also the virtual warehouse cache and query results cache, which are both used for performance optimization within Snowflake. All communication is encrypted in transit over public networks and even within the Snowflake virtual private cloud for customers who use the Business Critical Edition.

Note   Advanced Encryption Standard (AES) is a symmetric encryption algorithm. The algorithm was developed by two Belgian cryptographers, Joan Daemen and Vincent Rijmen. AES was designed to be efficient in both hardware and software and supports a block length of 128 bits and key lengths of 128, 192, and 256 bits.

All files that are stored in Snowflake internal stage objects are automatically encrypted using either AES128 or AES256 strong encryption. Specific additions of Snowflake also provide periodic rekeying of encrypted data and support for customer-managed encryption keys.

Business Critical Edition of Snowflake allows us to use the Tri-Secret Secure feature. This encryption is achieved using *key wrapping,* which means using one key to lock up another. For example, if a user attempts to access encrypted data within Snowflake, the data must first be decrypted. To decrypt it, the data key is necessary, but the data key itself is also encrypted or wrapped and requires another key, which is the table key. Again, the table key is locked and requires yet another key, the account key, to unlock it. The account key is also locked and can be accessed using the root key that is stored in the hardware security model, or Amazon CloudHSM within the cloud provider in the case of an AWS implementation.

Amazon CloudHSM is a piece of hardware that is specialized for encryption. The account key would need to be passed into CloudHSM and unlocked by the root key. Then the hierarchy of table and data keys can be subsequently unlocked, and the unencrypted data can be returned to the user.

Encryption keys are rotated automatically for accounts running on certain editions of Snowflake. The entire process of rotating encryption keys is completed behind the scenes and is transparent to the end user. With key rotation, a new version of a key is created, and the previous version of this key is retired. The new version of the key is used to encrypt data, while the previous version of the key is retired and used only to decrypt data. In other words, with key rotation, new data gets fresh keys.

Snowflake takes security seriously, which is why the end-to-end encryption of data is a default feature of the service. Whether data is in flight between the customer and internal stage or at rest and stored in a Snowflake database table, the data is always in an encrypted state.

To protect data against loss, Snowflake leverages data redundancy implemented by the cloud infrastructure provider. Each cloud provider region is geographically dispersed to several data centers across several miles within the region. The cloud infrastructure within each region provides automatic synchronous replication of data to three different zones for redundancy, should one's own have a failure. The data is available from one of the other two zones in the region.

Security Validation

Snowflakes supports multiple compliances, as described in Table 8-1. This makes Snowflake is an attractive platform for the financial, government and health industries where there are high compliance standards.

Table 8-1. *Snowflake Security Validations*

Type	Description
SOC 2 Type II	Designed for service providers storing customer data in the cloud. It requires companies to establish and follow strict information security policies and procedures encompassing the security, availability, processing, integrity, and confidentiality of customer data.
HIPPA	Stands for Health Insurance Portability and Accountability Act. Passed in 1996, HIPAA is a federal law that sets a national standard to protect medical records and other personal health information.
PCI DSS	Stands for Payment Card Industry Data Security Standard. This standard sets the requirements for organizations and sellers to safely and securely accept, store, process, and transmit card holder data during credit card transactions to prevent fraud and data breaches.
CAIQ	Stands for the Consensus Assessments Initiative Questionnaire (CAIQ). This is a survey provided by the Cloud Security Alliance (CSA) for cloud consumers and auditors to assess the security capabilities of a cloud service provider.

Snowflake Audit and Logging

Application audit logs are also available for tracking activity within Snowflake. All activity against the Snowflake service is logged within the service's layer. To access this activity log, go to the History tab in the Snowflake web user interface. From this page, users can view each command that was attempted along with the user who attempted the command, when the action occurred, and whether it was successful. Figure 8-4 shows the History tab.

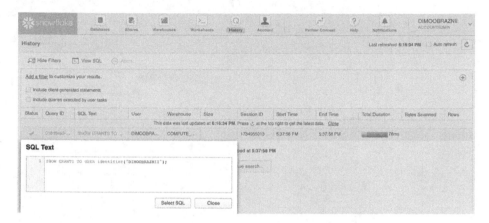

Figure 8-4. *Query History tab*

If you click the SQL text, a dialog will pop up with a success or failure message, as well as with actions to take to resolve any errors.

Another field in the activity log is Query ID. This ID can be used by Snowflake Support to look up a specific query instance for troubleshooting. Again, Snowflake personnel do not have access to customer data but can access metadata such as the query statement and query plan.

Clicking the Query ID field in the activity log will jump to the Query Profiler, allowing the user to view how the query optimizer worked and if there are any bottlenecks to resolve.

Query Profiler

When we work with data warehouse and business intelligence, often we have to deal with performance issues. To understand why our query or our report is slow, we should understand the mechanics of querying. Query Profiler helps us to spot typical mistakes in SQL query expressions to identify potential performance bottlenecks and improvement opportunities.

To access it, go to the History tab or Worksheets tab. If we navigate to the History tab and choose any query ID and then navigate to Profile, we will see the visual plan for query execution, as per Figure 8-5.

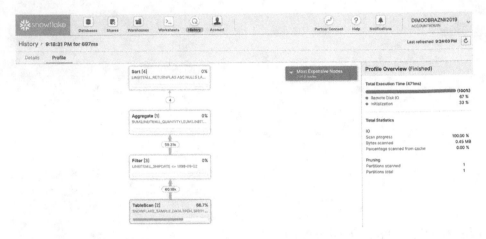

Figure 8-5. *Query Profiler*

Table 8-2 describes the key elements of the Query Profiler interface.

Table 8-2. *Key Elements of Query Profiler*

Element	Description
Steps	If the query was processed in multiple steps, you can toggle between each step.
Operator tree	The middle pane displays a graphical representation of all the operator nodes for the selected step, including the relationships between each operator node.
Node list	The middle pane includes a collapsible list of operator nodes by execution time.
Overview	The right pane displays an overview of the query profile. The display changes to operator details when an operator node is selected.

You can find more information about Query Profiler in the Snowflake documentation at `https://docs.snowflake.net/manuals/user-guide/ui-query-profile.html`.

Login History Audit Logs

Snowflake provides table functions for extracting audit log history from the metadata. The login history family of table functions can be used to look up user login history with various filters such as time range or specific user.

Additional SQL predicates can be used to further filter the results. This data remains available within the Snowflake metadata for seven days from the login event. Therefore, it can be extracted and loaded into a Snowflake schema or an external system such as a security information and event management system for more detailed audit history tracking. Table 8-3 describes the available tables and their purpose.

Table 8-3. *Login History Audit Functions*

Function	Description
LOGIN_HISTORY	Returns queries within a specified time range
LOGIN_HISTORY_BY_SESSION	Returns queries within a specified session and time range

Here is some example code for logging into the history audit logs:

```
--Retrieve up to the last 100 login events of the current user:
select *
from table(information_schema.login_history_by_user())
order by event_timestamp;
```

```
--Retrieve up to the last 1000 login events of the specified
user:
select *
from table(information_schema.login_history_by_user('USER1',
result_limit=>1000))
order by event_timestamp;
```

```
--Retrieve up to 100 login events of every user your current
role is allowed to monitor in the last hour:
select *
from table(information_schema.login_history(dateadd('hours',-1,
current_timestamp()),current_timestamp()))
order by event_timestamp;
```

Query History Audit Logs

The query logs in Snowflake can also be queried and extracted, just like the login history logs. The information in the query history family of functions is similar to the web user interface's History tab output. The query history can be filtered by time range, by session user, or even by specific warehouse query. Query history is also available only for seven days. So, for extended query history tracking, it is recommended you export the data to an external system or Snowflake table. Table 8-4 describes the available functions and their purpose.

Table 8-4. *Query History Audit Log Functions*

Function	Description
QUERY_HISTORY	Returns queries within a specified time range
QUERY_HISTORY_BY_SESSION	Returns queries within a specified session and time range
QUERY_HISTORY_BY_USER	Returns queries submitted by a specified user within a specified time range
QUERY_HISTORY_BY_DATAWAREHOUSE	Returns queries executed by a specified warehouse within a specified time range

Here is some example code for query history audit logs:

```
--Retrieve up to the last 100 queries run in the current
session:
select *
from table(information_schema.query_history_by_session())
order by start_time;
```

```
--Retrieve up to the last 100 queries run by the current user
(or run by any user on any warehouse on which the current user
has the MONITOR privilege):
```

```
select *
from table(information_schema.query_history())
order by start_time;

--Retrieve up to the last 100 queries run in the past hour by
the current user (or run by any user on any warehouse on which
the current user has the MONITOR privilege):
select *
from table(information_schema.query_history(dateadd('hours',-1,
current_timestamp()),current_timestamp()))
order by start_time;
```

Penetration Testing

Penetration tests are an integral part of Snowflake's ongoing testing of security controls and procedures. Seven to ten tests are performed each year to ensure no new holes or flaws arise in security. If a vulnerability is found, the security team will log and track it to closure. The results of these penetration tests are available to customers under NDA with Snowflake.

You can find more information about penetration testing in the article "Snowflake: Serious about security" by Susan Walsh at `https://www.snowflake.com/blog/snowflake-seriously-serious-security/`.

Summary

In this chapter, we briefly covered the key Snowflake security features in the following areas:

- Network/site access

- Account/user authentication

- Object security

- Data security

- Security validation

- Audit and logging

For each category, Snowflake provides extensive online documentation.

In the next chapter, you will learn about Snowflake's unique capabilities of working with semistructured data formats like JSON, XML, and AVRO.

CHAPTER 9

Working with Semistructured Data

Nowadays, companies buy and use many different systems from different companies. Eventually, data engineers face the problem of supporting different data formats for building analytical solutions and maintaining data sources. Data scientists face issues related to delivering valuable insight from semistructured data.

Historically, to load semistructured data into a relational repository, it was necessary to convert it to another format. However, with the NoSQL[1] revolution, such databases were used in conjunction with relational databases. Ultimately, relational engines began to support semistructured data.

Another concept that came from big data was the so-called schema-on-read approach. You first load the data as it is without thinking about the schema, and then when data already in the database, you working with this and define schema. A Snowflake database is a full ANSI SQL RDBMS that supports SQL for semistructured data while applying the schema-on-read[2] approach. In addition, Snowflake Support automatically converts data into column storage that is better suited for analytical workloads.

---

[1]https://en.wikipedia.org/wiki/NoSQL

[2]https://www.techopedia.com/definition/30153/schema-on-read

© Dmitry Anoshin, Dmitry Shirokov, Donna Strok 2020
D. Anoshin et al., *Jumpstart Snowflake*, https://doi.org/10.1007/978-1-4842-5328-1_9

In this chapter, you will learn about how Snowflake works with different formats. We will cover the following topics:

- Working with JSON, XML, and AVRO

- Working with ORC and Parquet

Supported File Formats

Snowflake supports many popular data formats. Table 9-1 lists some of the platforms that are integrated with Snowflake.

Snowflake provides the following for working with semistructured data:

- Storage engine that supports the most common formats and internal optimization storage processes

- Flexible schema data types and the ability to track changes

- SQL access for this data

For example, most REST[3] services use JSON. This is in contrast to the majority of legacy enterprise-level integration services that use XML to exchange data between corporate applications. If you use Hadoop or S3, you have worked with column-based formats before.

---

[3]https://en.wikipedia.org/wiki/Representational_state_transfer

Table 9-1. *Snowflake-Supported File Formats*

Format	Description
JSON	JSON[4] is a lightweight data-interchange format based on JavaScript.
AVRO	AVRO[5] is a data serialization format based on binary JSON.
ORC	Optimized Row Columnar (ORC[6]) is column-oriented[7] format originally developed for Apache Hive.
Parquet	Parquet[8] is the most used column-based format that came from the Hadoop ecosystem.
XML	Extensible Markup Language (XML[9]) is a markup language.

Advanced Data Types

In Snowflake the primary universal data type is VARIANT. You have to use it for working with semistructured data such as XML, JSON, AVRO, Parquet, and ORC. For high efficiency and performance, the Snowflake engine stores binary representations that support semistructured data using column-oriented storage with compression.

This process is completely transparent to the end user. The VARIANT type is a universal container that can store other types including OBJECT and ARRAY. There is a restriction on the maximum size of an object in compressed form, and it should not exceed 16 MB.

Any type of data in Snowflake can be converted to a VARIANT type. The database uses explicit and implicit type conversions. For explicit

---

[4]www.json.org/

[5]https://avro.apache.org/

[6]https://orc.apache.org/

[7]https://en.wikipedia.org/wiki/Column-oriented_DBMS

[8]http://parquet.apache.org/

[9]https://en.wikipedia.org/wiki/XML

conversions, use the functions TO_VARIANT(<expr>) or <expr>::VARIANT, where <expr> is an expression of any data type. Implicit conversion is used when you do not explicitly indicate this; for example, this happens when comparing data with different data types. For example, var:json_path >= 7 is cast to var:json_path >= 7::VARIANT.

Note   The VARIANT null value is distinct from the SQL NULL value. VARIANT null is real value that may be in semistructured data instead of SQL NULL. Use the test function IS_NULL_VALUE[10] to distinguish them.

In addition to type VARIANT, there are two more types.

- OBJECT is a key-value pair, where the key is a nonempty string and the value is a written value of the VARIANT type.

- ARRAY is an array, where the index is an integer (from 0 to 2^31-1), and values have the VARIANT type.

The steps for working with these types of data follow:

1. Create a file format and load the file into Snowflake.

2. Create a table with a column type of VARIANT, OBJECT, or ARRAY.

3. Parse JSON or XML using Snowflake SQL extension functions,[11] e.g., PARSE_JSON or PARSE_XML.

---

[10]https://docs.snowflake.net/manuals/sql-reference/functions/is_null_value.html

[11]https://docs.snowflake.net/manuals/sql-reference/functions-semistructured.html

4. Extract values from a structure and determine the data types using specific SQL functions, e.g., FLATTEN or GET.

5. Convert a structure to a lateral view using the LATERAL function.

6. Work with relational views as usual.

Working with XML

One of the most used formats for exchanging between companies is the XML format.

This format is often used in the world of enterprises as the main format for exchanging information between corporate services.

For instance, let's use an open database called US New York Demographic Statistics. The database provides statistical information about the residents of New York. Using a specific request[12] to this database, we can download the sample in XML format.

Listing 9-1 shows an example of the response of the RESTful service from the sample request.

Listing 9-1. Example of XML

```
<response>
<row>
<row _id="row-abpe~s85f-zkcw" _uuid="00000000-0000-0000-00000"
_position="0" _address="https://data.cityofnewyork.us/resource/
kku6-nxdu/row-abpe~s85f-zkcw">
<jurisdiction_name>10001</jurisdiction_name>
```

---

[12]https://data.cityofnewyork.us/api/views/kku6-nxdu/rows. xml?accessType=DOWNLOAD

```
<count_participants>44</count_participants>
<count_female>22</count_female>
<percent_female>0.5</percent_female>
<count_male>22</count_male>
<percent_male>0.5</percent_male>
<count_gender_unknown>0</count_gender_unknown>
<percent_gender_unknown>0</percent_gender_unknown>
<count_gender_total>44</count_gender_total>
<percent_gender_total>100</percent_gender_total>
<count_pacific_islander>0</count_pacific_islander>
<percent_pacific_islander>0</percent_pacific_islander>
<count_hispanic_latino>16</count_hispanic_latino>
<percent_hispanic_latino>0.36</percent_hispanic_latino>
<count_american_indian>0</count_american_indian>
<percent_american_indian>0</percent_american_indian>
<count_asian_non_hispanic>3</count_asian_non_hispanic>
```

With this example, you can see that the structure of an XML file contains the following:

- Field *message* that contains basic response information

- Summary of request, including the following:

    - Tag *response*, including the tag row

    - Tag *row*, which contains attribute tags

    - Many attribute tags with *data*

Snowflake allows you to load such data directly into the database while applying encryption on the fly and provides a set of functions that extends the standard SQL, which makes it easy to work within the structure of XML documents.

In other words, for querying any XML file, we could use special built-in functions that extend ANSI SQL as follows:

- The table function LATERAL FLATTEN[13] for extracting data from a structure

- The $ and @ operators to access the root element and attributes

- The XMLGET[14] function for extracting the name of a tag from an XML element

---

USING SNOWFLAKE SQL FOR XML

Let's look at how to work with XML in Snowflake:

1. Log into your Snowflake's account and choose the Worksheets tab.

2. Choose your sample databases and warehouse using DML, as follows:

```
use warehouse "COMPUTE_WH_TEST";
use "DEMO_DB"."PUBLIC";
```

3. Create a table called demo_xml with the VARIANT attribute by using a DDL statement.

```
create or replace table demo_xml (val variant);
```

4. Download the XML file onto your computer using the request in the previous link.

---

[13]https://docs.snowflake.net/manuals/sql-reference/functions/flatten.html

[14]https://docs.snowflake.net/manuals/sql-reference/functions/xmlget.html

5. Open the Snowflake UI and choose the Databases tab. Click the table and then click the Load Data button. See Figure 9-1.

Databases › DEMO_DB › DEMO_XML (PUBLIC)
Tables
Views
Schemas
Stages
File Formats
Load Table
Column Name
Ordinal
Type
VAL
1
VARIANT

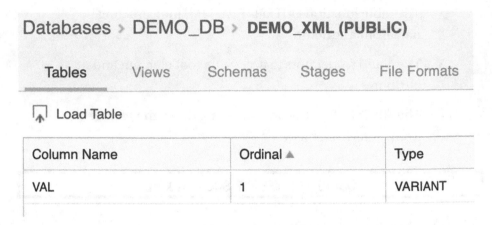

Figure 9-1. *Loading data into the table using the Snowflake UI*

6. In the window that opens, select your Snowflake warehouse, as shown in Figure 9-2.

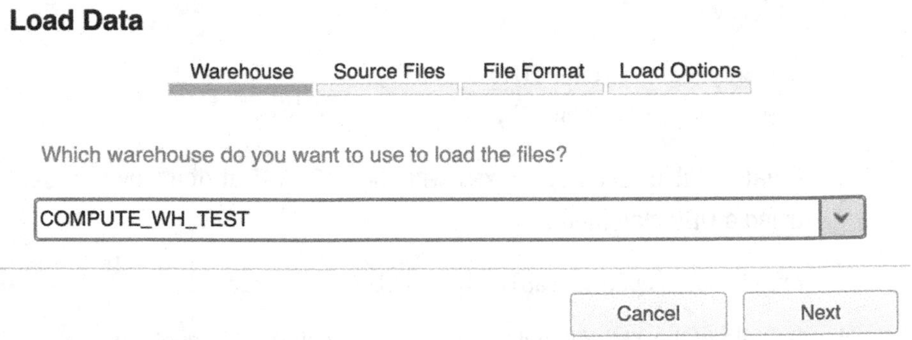

Load Data
Warehouse
Source Files
File Format
Load Options
Which warehouse do you want to use to load the files?
COMPUTE_WH_TEST
Cancel
Next

Figure 9-2. *Choosing the warehouse*

7. Choose your XML file and download it into the Snowflake cloud. See Figure 9-3.

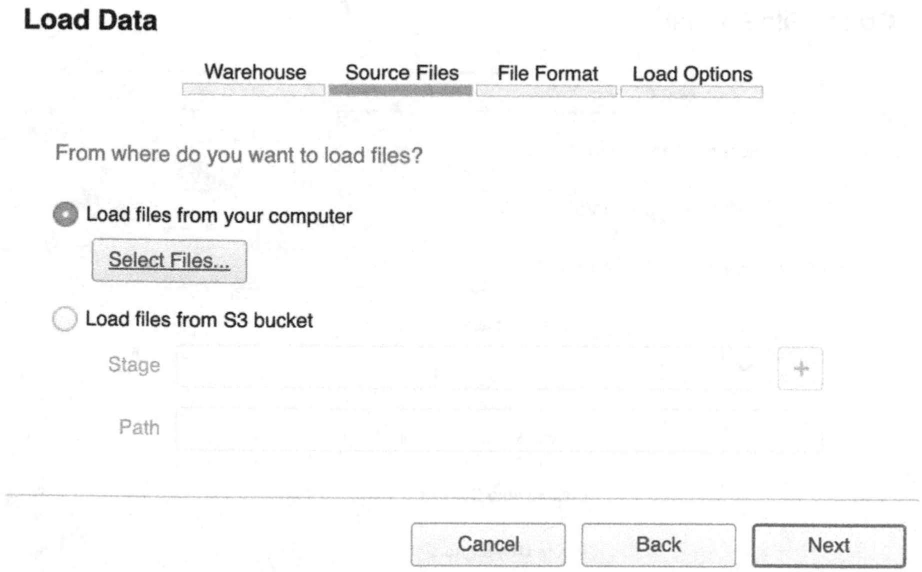

Load Data

Warehouse	Source Files	File Format	Load Options

From where do you want to load files?

○ Load files from your computer

> Select Files...

○ Load files from S3 bucket

Stage [   ] ⌄ [+]

Path [   ]

[Cancel]   [Back]   [Next]

Figure 9-3. *Choosing the source file for downloading into Snowflake*

8. Create a new file format for the table. See Figure 9-4.

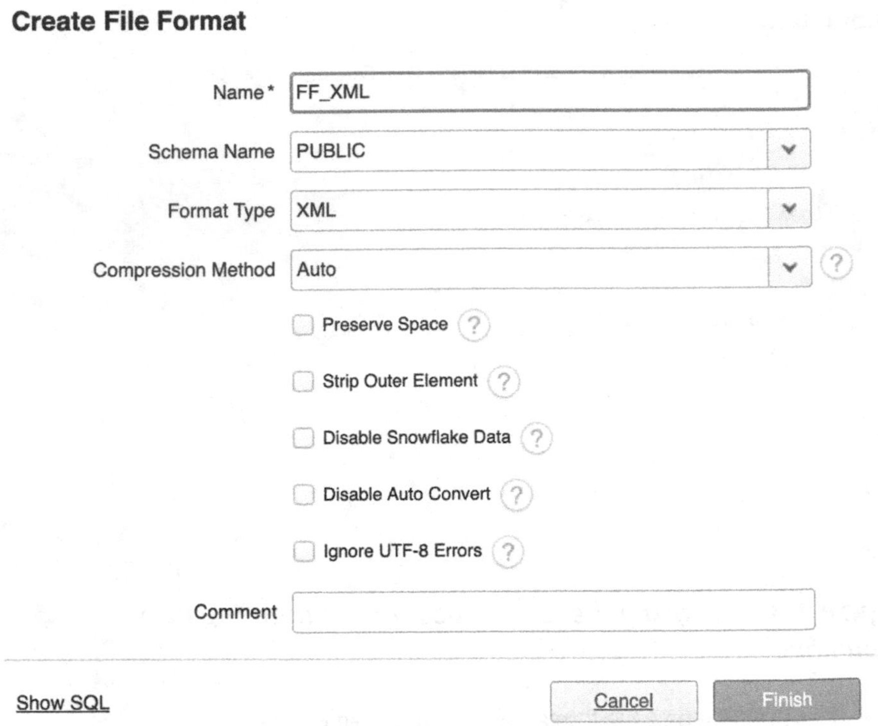

Create File Format

Name*	FF_XML
Schema Name	PUBLIC ⌄
Format Type	XML ⌄
Compression Method	Auto ⌄ ⑦
	☐ Preserve Space ⑦
	☐ Strip Outer Element ⑦
	☐ Disable Snowflake Data ⑦
	☐ Disable Auto Convert ⑦
	☐ Ignore UTF-8 Errors ⑦
Comment	

Show SQL   Cancel   Finish

Figure 9-4. *Creating a new file format into Snowflake*

9. Choose the FF_XML format. See Figure 9-5.

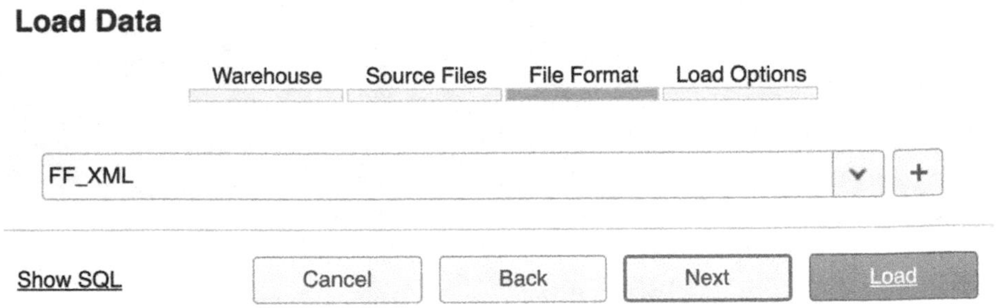

Load Data

Warehouse   Source Files   File Format   Load Options

FF_XML   ⌄ +

Show SQL   Cancel   Back   Next   Load

Figure 9-5. *Selecting a file format*

10. Upload the sample file into Snowflake using Load Options by default. See Figure 9-6.

Load Data

Warehouse	Source Files	File Format	Load Options

What should the load do if it encounters an error while parsing a file?

- ○ Do not load any data in the file
- ◉ Stop loading, rollback and return the error
- ○ Do not load any data in the file if the error count exceeds:

    Threshold   0

- ○ Continue loading valid data from the file

Show SQL   Cancel   Back   Load

Figure 9-6. *Selecting Load Options*

11. Check the data by using a SQL statement. See Figure 9-7.

```
select * from demo_xml;
```

Figure 9-7. *XML data in the table*

12. Try to access the root element using the $ operator. See Figure 9-8.

```
select val:"$" from demo_xml;
```

Row	VAL:"$"
1	\<row> \<row _address="https://data.cityofnewyork.us/resource/kku6-nxdu/row-abpe~s85f-zkcw" .

Figure 9-8. *Applying the $ operator on the XML data in the table*

13. Try to extract the row attribute using the XMLGET function. See
    Figure 9-9.

    ```
    select XMLGET(val, 'row',0):"$" from demo_xml;
    ```

Details

```
 1  [
 2    {
 3      "$": [
 4        {
 5          "$": 10001,
 6          "@": "jurisdiction_name"
 7        },
 8        {
 9          "$": 44,
10          "@": "count_participants"
11        },
12        {
13          "$": 22
```

Done

Figure 9-9. *Applying the XMLGET function to the ROW attribute*

Figure 9-9 shows the query result, which is a hierarchy in which the
name of the tag is written to @ and the value of the tag is written to $.

14. Extract an array of values using the LATERAL FLATTEN table
    function with the to_array function, as shown in Listing 9-2.
    See Figure 9-10.

Listing 9-2. Extracting Values from an Array of the Table

```
select
xml_doc_val.index,
xml_doc_val.value
from demo_xml,
LATERAL FLATTEN(to_array(demo_xml.val:"$" )) xml_doc,
LATERAL FLATTEN(to_array(xml_doc.VALUE:"$" )) xml_doc_val;
```

Row	INDEX	VALUE
1	0	<row _address="https://data.cityofnewyork.us/resource/kku6-nxdu/row-abpe~s85f-zkcw" _id="row-abpe~s85f-zkcw"
2	1	<row _address="https://data.cityofnewyork.us/resource/kku6-nxdu/row-hnhe_au83-ufuq" _id="row-hnhe_au83-ufuq"
3	2	<row _address="https://data.cityofnewyork.us/resource/kku6-nxdu/row-aupu.kqkr~6w42" _id="row-aupu.kqkr~6w42"

Figure 9-10. *Applying the LATERAL FLATTEN table function to the table*

In Listing 9-2, in the query, LATERAL FLATTEN is used twice sequentially to extract a portion of the XML document and convert it into rows.

15. To complete the conversion of an array of values into a table view, modify the query as shown in Listing 9-3. See Figure 9-11.

Listing 9-3. Creating a View Based on Extracting Values from the Array of the Table

```
create view stats_by_zip AS
select
    XMLGET( xml_doc_val.value, 'jurisdiction_name'
    ):"$" as "Jurisdiction_Name",
    XMLGET( xml_doc_val.value, 'count_participants'
    ):"$" as "Count_Participants",
    XMLGET( xml_doc_val.value, 'count_female' ):"$"
    as "Count_Female",
```

159

```
    XMLGET( xml_doc_val.value, 'count_male' ):"$"
    as "Count_Male"
from demo_xml,
LATERAL FLATTEN(to_array(demo_xml.val:"$" )) xml_doc,
LATERAL FLATTEN(to_array(xml_doc.VALUE:"$" )) xml_doc_val;
select * from stats_by_zip;
```

Row	jurisdiction name	count_participants	count_female	count_male
1	10001	44	22	22
2	10002	35	19	16
3	10003	1	1	0
4	10004	0	0	0

Figure 9-11. *Creating a lateral view from the XML table*

In Listing 9-3, the query is similar to the previous one, and the XMLGET function is used, which retrieves values and generates values by columns.

16. Let's create a new view using the previous query and add some names of neighborhoods from the site, as shown in Listing 9-4.[15]

Listing 9-4. Extracting Values from the Array of the Table

```
create or replace table dic_zip_neighborhoods (zip_code
    string(5), name string(35));

insert into dic_zip_neighborhoods
values('10001','Chelsea and Clinton'),
  ('10002','Lower East Side'),
  ('10003','Lower East Side'),
  ('10004','Lower Manhattan')
  ..
  ;
```

---

[15]https://www.health.ny.gov/statistics/cancer/registry/appendix/
neighborhoods.htm

```
create view stats_by_zip_with_neighborhoods AS
select s.Jurisdiction_Name,
       d.name as Neighborhoods,
       s.Count_Participants,
       s.Count_Female,
       s.Count_Male
from stats_by_zip as s
left outer join dic_zip_neighborhoods as d
 on trim(s.Jurisdiction_Name::string) = d.zip_code
select * from stats_by_zip_with_neighborhoods;
```

In the view stats_by_zip_with_neighborhoods, we combined a regular relational table and view based on XML data, applying the schema and extracting only the necessary attributes on the fly. This view can easily be connected to the BI tool.

Working with JSON

These days, the JSON format is the most popular format for exchanging data. Let's take a look at how Snowflake works with JSON. Let's take a sample of financial data using a provider called "World Trading Data."[16] Perform a request[17] to find out information about the companies Apple, Microsoft, and HSBC Holding.

Listing 9-5 shows an example of the response of the RESTful service on the sample request.

---

[16]https://www.worldtradingdata.com
[17]https://api.worldtradingdata.com/api/v1/stock?symbol=AAPL,MSFT,HSBA.L&api_token=demo

Listing 9-5. Example of JSON Data from NASDAQ

```json
{
  "message": "This request..",
  "symbols_requested": 3,
  "symbols_returned": 3,
  "data": [
    {
      "symbol": "AAPL",
      "name": "Apple Inc.",
      "currency": "USD",
      "price": "202.73",
      "price_open": "201.41",
      "day_high": "203.13",
      "day_low": "201.36",
      "52_week_high": "233.47",
      "52_week_low": "142.00",
      "day_change": "1.18",
      "change_pct": "0.59",
      "close_yesterday": "201.55",
      "market_cap": "932776902656",
      "volume": "16682004",
      "volume_avg": "27522800",
      "shares": "4601079808",
      "stock_exchange_long": "NASDAQ Stock Exchange",
      "stock_exchange_short": "NASDAQ",
      "timezone": "EDT",
      "timezone_name": "America/New_York",
      "gmt_offset": "-14400",
      "last_trade_time": "2019-07-02 16:00:01"
    },
    {..},
```

```
    {..}
 ..
  ]
}
```

You can see that the response is a tree structure that contains the following:

- Field *message* that contains basic response information

- Summary of request including the following:

  - Attribute symbols_requested

  - Attribute symbols_returned

  - Attribute data that is a container for data

USING SNOWFLAKE SQL FOR JSON

Let's look at how to work with JSON in Snowflake.

1. Log into your Snowflake account and choose Worksheets.

2. Choose your sample databases and warehouse using DML, as follows:

   ```
   use warehouse "COMPUTE_WH_TEST";
   use "DEMO_DB"."PUBLIC";
   ```

3. Create the table stock_json by using the following DDL statement:

   ```
   create or replace table stock_json (val variant);
   ```

   val is a field with the type VARIANT.

4. Insert the sample JSON into Snowflake's table by using the
    parse_json function.

    ```
    insert into stock_json select parse_json('<JSON>');
    ```

    Replace the substitutions with the recent JSON code before executing.

5. Check the data into the table. See Figure 9-12.

    ```
    Select * from stock_json;
    ```

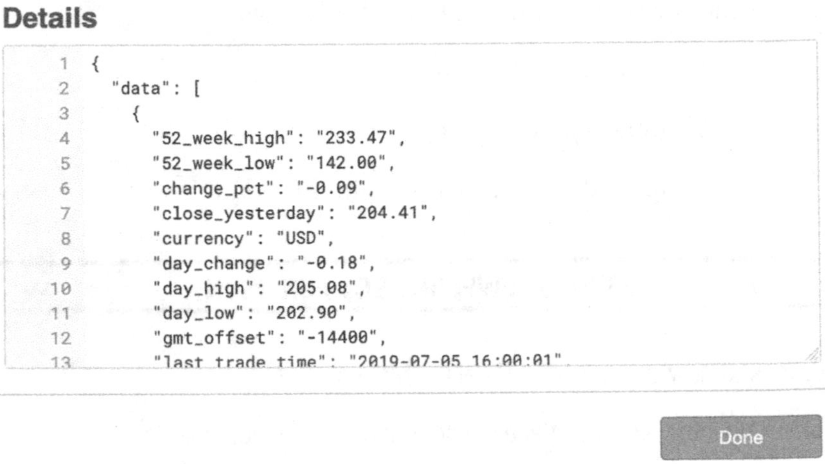

Details

```
 1  {
 2    "data": [
 3      {
 4        "52_week_high": "233.47",
 5        "52_week_low": "142.00",
 6        "change_pct": "-0.09",
 7        "close_yesterday": "204.41",
 8        "currency": "USD",
 9        "day_change": "-0.18",
10        "day_high": "205.08",
11        "day_low": "202.90",
12        "gmt_offset": "-14400",
13        "last_trade_time": "2019-07-05 16:00:01".
```

`Done`

Figure 9-12.   JSON data in the table

6. Use the notation `<field>:<attribute>[::type]` to extract
    data from a specific attribute, as shown in Listing 9-6. See
    Figure 9-13.

Note   Use the notation `<field>:<list>.<attribute>[::type]`
if you need to extract nested attributes but not from arrays.

Listing 9-6. Querying JSON by Using SQL

```
select val:message::string as msg,
   val:symbols_requested::int as smbl_rqstd,
val:symbols_returned::int as smbl_rtrnd
   from stock_json;
```

Row	MSG	SMBL_RQSTD	SMBL_RTRND
1	This request is f...	3	3

Figure 9-13. *Extracting attributes from the JSON structure*

Note   Unlike the behavior of ordinary relational databases, in Snowflake, the query will not fail if the schema accidently changes. For example, when an attribute is requested that is missing, it will simply return a NULL value.

---

7. For extracting nested elements from the array, use the built-in table function FLATTEN, as shown in Listing 9-7.[18] See Figure 9-14.

    ```
    table(flatten(<array>:<elements>))
    ```

Listing 9-7. Extracting Elements of Arrays of JSON by Using SQL

```
select f.*
    from stock_json s,
table(flatten(val:data)) f;
```

---

[18]https://docs.snowflake.net/manuals/sql-reference/functions/flatten.html

Row	SEQ	KEY	PATH	INDEX	VALUE	THIS
1	1	NULL	[0]	0	{ "52_week_high": "233....	[{ "52_week_high": "233...
2	1	NULL	[1]	1	{ "52_week_high": "736....	[{ "52_week_high": "233...
3	1	NULL	[2]	2	{ "52_week_high": "138....	[{ "52_week_high": "233...

Figure 9-14. *Applying the FLATTEN function to JSON*

In Listing 9-8, in the query, FLATTEN extract column names from val:data of the JSON document and converts it into rows.

8. To extract nested elements from the array, use the built-in table function FLATTEN: table(flatten(<array>:<elemen ts>)). See Figure 9-15.

Listing 9-8. *Extracting Elements of Arrays in JSON by Using SQL*

```
select
  s.val:message::string as msg,
  s.val:symbols_requested::int as smbl_rqstd,
  s.val:symbols_returned::int as smbl_rtrnd,
  f.value:symbol::string as smbl,
  f.value:name::string as smbl_name,
  f.value:currency::string as smbl_currency,
  f.value:price::float as prc
 from stock_json s,
table(flatten(val:data)) f
```

Row	MSG	SMBL_RQSTD	SMBL_RTRND	SMBL	SMBL_NAME	SMBL_CURRENCY	PRC
1	This request is for ...	3	3	AAPL	Apple Inc.	USD	204.23
2	This request is for ...	3	3	HSBA.L	HSBC Holdings plc	GBX	672.5
3	This request is for ...	3	3	MSFT	Microsoft Corporat...	USD	137.06

Figure 9-15. *Extracting attributes from the JSON structure*

Note   To count the number of elements in an array, you can use the function array_size(<array>:<elements>).

Working with AVRO

An AVRO file is serialized JSON with a schema. It is often used as a data transport format in Apache Kafka.

To work with the data from the AVRO file, you have to do the following:

1. Create a new stage for creating a new AVRO file format.

2. Upload the AVRO file into the stage in Snowflake to create a new file format.

3. Create a target table.

4. Copy the data from the file into the target table.

5. Query the data in the table using the Snowflake SQL extension.

6. To do this, you can use the Snowflake UI or a command.[19]

Additionally, you can use AVRO tools.[20] Specifically, you can use a Java package of specific tools for working with the AVRO format including doing serialization of some JSON files using AVRO schemas.

WORKING WITH AVRO

Let's look at how to work with AVRO in Snowflake:

1. On your local computer, create a new JSON sample file and save it as stock_sample2.json, as shown in Listing 9-9.

---

[19]https://docs.snowflake.net/manuals/sql-reference/sql/create-file-format.html

[20]http://mirrors.ocf.berkeley.edu/apache/avro/stable/java/

Listing 9-9. JSON Sample File

```
{"symbol":"AAPL","name":"Apple
   Inc.","price":201.41,"last_trade_time":
   1568579958}
{"symbol":"AAPL","name":"Apple
   Inc.","price":201.42,"last_trade_time":
   1568587158}
..
{"symbol":"HSBA.L","name":"HSBC
   Holding","price":826.33,"last_trade_time":
   1568587158}
{"symbol":"HSBA.L","name":"HSBC
   Holding","price":826.47,"last_trade_time":
   1568648358}
```

2. Create an Avro Schema for this sample file and save it as
   `stock_sample2.avsc`, as shown in Listing 9-10.

Listing 9-10. AVRO Schema File

```
{
  "type" : "record",
  "name" : "simple_stock_schema",
  "namespace" : "com.apress.snowflake_jumpstart.avro",
  "fields" : [ {
    "name" : "symbol",
    "type" : "string",
    "doc"  : "Symbol of the stock"
  }, {
    "name" : "name",
    "type" : "string",
    "doc"  : "Name of the stock"
  }, {
    "name" : "price",
```

```
    "type" : "float",
    "doc"  : "Price of the stock"
  }, {
    "name" : "last_trade_time",
    "type" : "long",
    "doc"  : "Last trade time. Time Unix epoch time in seconds"
  } ],
  "doc:" : "A basic schema for storing stock messages"
}
```

3. Download the last version of the AVRO tools and generate an AVRO sample file, as shown in Listing 9-11.

Listing 9-11. AVRO File Generation

```
java -jar ./avro-tools-1.9.0.jar fromjson --schema-file stock_
sample2.avsc stock_sample2.json > stock_sample2.avro
```

Snowflake supports Snappy[21] compression, so you can add this option:

```
--codec snappy
```

4. Create the target table and the stage for the AVRO file in the table and save it as `meta_avro.sql`, as shown in Listing 9-12.

Listing 9-12. Creating Metadata for Loading an AVRO File

```
use warehouse "COMPUTE_WH_TEST";
use "DEMO_DB"."PUBLIC";
create or replace table c (val variant);

create or replace file format myavroformat
  type = 'AVRO';

create or replace stage my_avro_stage
  file_format = myavroformat;
```

---

[21]https://en.wikipedia.org/wiki/Snappy_(compression)

5. Run the script.

```
snowsql -c cc -f meta_avro.sql
```

Here, cc is your connection label in the config file of snowsql.

6. Create the script for uploading the AVRO data file. Save the script as put_avro_file.sql, as shown in Listing 9-13.

Listing 9-13. Uploading the Data and Copying It into the Target Table

```
use warehouse "COMPUTE_WH_TEST";
use "DEMO_DB"."PUBLIC";

put file:///Path/to/file/stock_sample2.avro @my_avro_stage auto_
compress=true;

copy into demo_avro
  from @my_avro_stage/stock_sample2.avro.gz
  file_format = (format_name = myavroformat)
  on_error = 'skip_file';
```

7. Upload the file into the Snowflake cloud.

```
snowsql -c cc -f put_avro_file.sql
```

8. Now we can check the data in the table, as shown in Listing 9-14. See Figure 9-16.

Listing 9-14. Requesting the Data Loaded from an AVRO File

```
select val:symbol::string as symbol,
    val:name::string as name,
    TO_TIMESTAMP(val:last_trade_time::number) as last_trade_time
    val:price::number(10,2) as price
  from demo_avro;
```

Row	SYMBOL	NAME	LAST_TRADE_TIME	PRICE
1	AAPL	Apple Inc.	2019-09-15 20:39:18.000	201.41
2	AAPL	Apple Inc.	2019-09-15 22:39:18.000	201.42
3	AAPL	Apple Inc.	2019-09-16 15:39:18.000	201.44
4	HSBA.L	HSBC Holding	2019-09-15 20:39:18.000	826.21
5	HSBA.L	HSBC Holding	2019-09-15 22:39:18.000	826.33
6	HSBA.L	HSBC Holding	2019-09-16 15:39:18.000	826.47

Figure 9-16. *Loaded data from AVRO file in the table*

Working with Parquet

A Parquet file is a compressed column-oriented binary file. It is used to store big data with an analytical workload.

To work with the data in a Parquet file, you do the following:

1. Create a new stage for creating a new Parquet file format.

2. Upload the Parquet file into the stage in Snowflake where you have to create a new file format.

3. Create a target table.

4. Copy the data from the file in the stage to the target table using mapping fields.

5. Query the data in the table.

Use a similar approach for working with ORC files.

WORKING WITH PARQUET

Let's look at how to work with Parquet in Snowflake.

Since we do not have a Parquet file, let's make it from a CSC file using Python with the Pandas[22] and PyArrow[23] libraries. Pandas is a popular library for data manipulation, and it can read our comma-separated file. PyArrow is a Python interface for Apache Arrow that is a cross-language development platform for in-memory data, which can also operate with different types of data including Parquet.

1. On your local computer, create a new CSV sample file and save it as `stock_sample3.csv`, as shown in Listing 9-15.

Listing 9-15. CSV Sample File

```
symbol,name,price,last_trade_time
"AAPL","Apple Inc.",201.42,1568587158
"AAPL","Apple Inc.",201.41,1568579958
"AAPL","Apple Inc.",201.44,1568648358
"MSFT","Microsoft",136.01,1568579958
"MSFT","Microsoft",136.92,1568587158
..
"HSBA.L","HSBC Holding",826.47,1568648358
```

2. Let's install the necessary libraries.

    ```
    pip install pandas pyarrow
    ```

3. Make a simple Python script that reads the CSV file and writes it in Parquet format. Save the file as `csv_to_parquet.py`, as shown in Listing 9-16.

---

[22]https://pandas.pydata.org/
[23]https://arrow.apache.org/docs/python/

Listing 9-16. Transforming Data from CSV to Parquet

```python
import pandas as pd
import pyarrow as pa
import pyarrow.parquet as pq

csv_file = 'stock_sample3.csv'
parquet_file = 'stock_sample3.parquet'
# read data from CSV file
df = pd.read_csv(csv_file)
# check it
print(df.dtypes)
print(df.to_string())
    # write the data in parquet file
table = pa.Table.from_pandas(df)
pq.write_table(table, parquet_file, compression='snappy')
```

4. Create the target table and the stage for the Parquet file. Save the script as meta_parquet.sql, as shown in Listing 9-17.

Listing 9-17. Creating Metadata for Loading the Parquet File

```sql
use warehouse "COMPUTE_WH_TEST";
use "DEMO_DB"."PUBLIC";

create or replace table demo_parquet (
  symbol varchar,
  name   varchar,
  price  number(10,2),
  last_trade_time timestamp
);

create or replace file format myparquetformat
  type = 'PARQUET';

create or replace stage my_parquet_stage
  file_format = myparquetformat;
```

5. Run the script.

```
snowsql -c cc -f meta_parquet.sql
```

cc is your connection label in the config file of snowsql.

6. Create the script for uploading the Parquet file. Save the script as put_parquet_file.sql, as shown in Listing 9-18.

Listing 9-18. Uploading the Data and Copying It into the Target Table

```
use warehouse "COMPUTE_WH_TEST";
use "DEMO_DB"."PUBLIC";

put file:///Path/to/File/stock_sample3.parquet @my_parquet_stage
auto_compress=true;

# extract and mapping values than copy data in the table
copy into demo_parquet
    from (select
            $1:symbol::varchar,
            $1:name::varchar,
            $1:price::number(10,2),
            to_timestamp($1:last_trade_time::number)
            from @my_parquet_stage/stock_sample3.parquet
        )
    file_format = (format_name = myparquetformat)
    on_error = 'skip_file'
    ;
```

7. Run the script for uploading and checking the result. See Figure 9-17.

```
snowsql -c cc -f put_parquet_file.sql
```

Table: DEMO_DB.PUBLIC.DEMO_PARQUET   Data   Details

Row	SYMBOL	NAME	PRICE	LAST_TRADE_TIME
1	AAPL	Apple Inc.	201.42	2019-09-15 22:39:18.000
2	AAPL	Apple Inc.	201.41	2019-09-15 20:39:18.000
3	AAPL	Apple Inc.	201.44	2019-09-16 15:39:18.000
4	MSFT	Microsoft	136.01	2019-09-15 20:39:18.000
5	MSFT	Microsoft	136.92	2019-09-15 22:39:18.000

Figure 9-17. *Loaded data from the Parquet file in the table*

Summary

In this chapter, we briefly covered how Snowflake can work with different data formats. Moreover, you learned about which semistructured data formats are supported in Snowflake and saw how this is done in practice by running the examples with JSON, XML, AVRO, and Parquet.

In the next chapter, you will learn about Snowflake's data sharing capabilities.

CHAPTER 10

Secure Data Sharing

Data sharing inside and outside the organization is one of the most technically challenging tasks facing modern companies today.

Snowflake provides special features for distributing and sharing corporate data.

In most cases, data providers must upload the data from a database, encrypt each of the data sets, and then upload statistical data sets via FTP[1] for distribution.

Then consumers have to download the data and painstakingly restore it by copying it into their databases. There are other tools for sharing on a cloud or on-premise platform, but they require ETL.[2] E-mail exchange is also possible, but it is slow and limited to a small file and also often leads to an overflow of your e-mail account. The Snowflake company rethought the data exchange process and proposed a new approach based on the cloud architecture as a modern tool for distributing data.

Your data may be stored in Snowflake for some time. If you have changed or even deleted some of it, you can always request a previous state from a certain point in time, which is extremely convenient when working with data.

In this chapter, we will cover the following topics:

---

[1]File Transfer Protocol, https://en.wikipedia.org/wiki/
File_Transfer_Protocol

[2]Extract, transform, load https://en.wikipedia.org/wiki/
Extract,_transform,_load

© Dmitry Anoshin, Dmitry Shirokov, Donna Strok 2020
D. Anoshin et al., *Jumpstart Snowflake*, https://doi.org/10.1007/978-1-4842-5328-1_10

- How to securely share your data using Snowflake

- How to work with versions of objects

Secure Data Sharing

The following are the key Snowflake data sharing benefits:

- No data movement, no data copying

- Instant access to shared data

- The ability to share and grant access to other companies to use your database

- Updates reflected instantly

- Limited access to the row-level data by using secure views

It is necessary to understand that in the process of sharing there is no real copying of data. Therefore, the *data consumer* pays only for the computing service but does not pay for the storage of this data, since physically the data remains stored with the data provider. Since the information is not actually transferred, consumers get an instant update when the provider changes the data. A single *data provider* may have multiple data consumers, both within the company and with external consumers. Similarly, data consumers may have access to multiple providers, thereby forming a network of providers and consumers.

Let's see how it works. The data sharing feature provides the ability to share database objects between Snowflake's accounts within a region by using a specific share object. Such objects can be tables, secure views, and secure UDFs.[3] The data provider creates a share object, and the data consumer uses this object for access.

Essentially, a *share* is an object that contains information about the following:

- Permissions that provide access to the provider's database and selected objects

- Consumer database and objects that are shared

Often there is a situation where you have a base table, and you need to organize access to only part of the records of this table. The best practice is to use *secure views*.

The data sharing feature in Snowflake works only between Snowflake accounts. If you want to grant access to the outside world, you will need to use a *reader account*.[4]

A provider account can create reader accounts for those consumers who are not customers of Snowflake. See Figure 10-1.

---

[3]https://docs.snowflake.net/manuals/sql-reference/user-defined-functions.html

[4]https://docs.snowflake.net/manuals/user-guide/data-sharing-reader-create.html

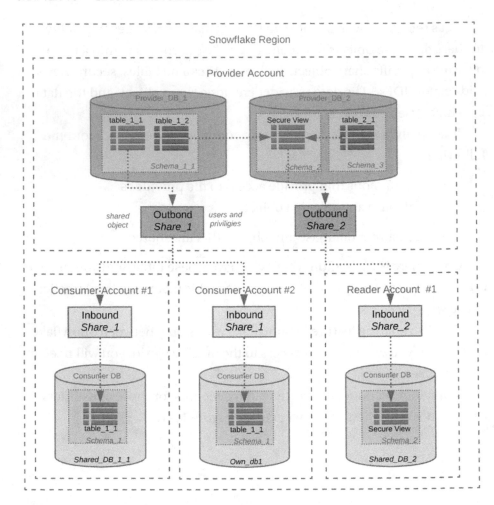

Figure 10-1. *Snowflake data sharing*

Table 10-1 highlights the steps of the data sharing process in Figure 10-1.

Table 10-1. *Data Sharing Process*

Step	Description
1	The provider account creates a share object called `Share_1` on the database `Provider_DB_1` and grants access to selected objects in `table_1_1`.
2	The consumer account creates the read-only database from the `Share_1` object. Then, all shared objects are available to consumers. In Figure 10-1, the accounts are called Customer Account #1 and Customer Account #2.
4	If consumers do not have an account in Snowflake, the provider can create a reader account for them. In Figure 10-1, this is implemented for the object `Share_2`.
5	Shared objects can be a table (like `table_1_1`), but the best practice is to use a secure view. A view can include multiple private tables from various databases.
6	In a secure view, as an option, we can use control data access by rows. For this, we have to create a table in which there will be a mapping of a group of records on users.
7	The consumer account grants permissions according to role-based access control.

Secure Table Sharing

If you have a table, then for organizing access to the table, you need to perform only three necessary steps.

1. Create a share object.

2. Add a table name to the share and grant privileges.

3. Add a consumer account to the share object.

4. Log into a consumer account.

5. Add the available share to the account and query the shared tables.

Let's do an example.

EXAMPLE WITH SHARING TABLE

Let's look at how to share a table in practice:

1. Log into your Snowflake account (the provider account).

2. Switch to a worksheet and run the code in Listing 10-1. See Figure 10-2.

Listing 10-1. Creating Sample Data

```
use role sysadmin;
create database samples;
create schema samples.finance;
create or replace table samples.finance.stocks_data (
    id int,
    symbol string,
    date date,
    time time(9),
    bid_price float,
        ask_price float,
        bid_cnt int,
        ask_cnt int
    );

insert into samples.finance.stocks_data
  values(1,'TDC',dateadd(day,  -1,current_date()), '10:15:00', 36.3,
  36.0, 10, 10),
```

```
(2,'TDC', dateadd(month,-2,current_date()), '11:14:00',
36.5, 36.2, 10, 10),
(3,'ORCL', dateadd(day, -1,current_date()), '11:15:00',
57.8, 59.9, 13, 13),
(4,'ORCL', dateadd(month,-2,current_date()), '09:11:00',
57.3, 57.9, 12, 12),
(5,'TSLA', dateadd(day, -1,current_date()), '11:01:00',
255.2, 256.4, 22, 22),
(6,'TSLA', dateadd(month, -2,current_date()), '11:13:00',
255.2, 255.7, 23, 23);

select * from samples.finance.stocks_data;
```

ROWID	SYMBOL	DATE	TIME	BID_PRICE	ASK_PRICE	BID_CNT	ASK_CNT
1	TDC	2019-07-18	10:15:00	36.3	36	10	10
2	TDC	2019-05-19	11:14:00	36.5	36.2	10	10
3	ORCL	2019-07-18	11:15:00	57.8	59.9	13	13
4	ORCL	2019-05-19	09:11:00	57.3	57.9	12	12
5	TSLA	2019-07-18	11:01:00	255.2	256.4	22	22
6	TSLA	2019-05-19	11:13:00	255.2	255.7	23	23

Figure 10-2. *Table with stock data*

In Listing 10-1 we did the following:

- We created a new database called samples and a schema called samples.finance.

- We created a sample table called samples.finance. stocks_data and filled it with values.

- We created a share object and provided access to another account.

Now see Listing 10-2.

Listing 10-2. Creating a Share and Granting Permissions to a
New Account

```
use role accountadmin;
create or replace share stocks_share;
show shares;
grant usage on database samples to share stocks_share;
grant usage on schema samples.finance to share stocks_share;
grant select on table samples.finance.stocks_data to share
stocks_share;
   show grants to share stocks_share;

alter share stocks_share add accounts=<consumer_account>;
```

In Listing 10-2 we did the following:

- We created a shared object called stocks_share and
  a schema called samples.finance. You can see the
  metadata of the share object in Figure 10-3.

Row	↓ created_on	kind	name	database_name	to	owner	comment
3	2019-07-17 17:0...	OUTBOUND	⟩⟩⟩⟩ ⟩⟩⟩.STOCKS_SHARE	SAMPLES		ACCOUNTADMIN	

Figure 10-3. *Metadata of share object*

- We granted privileges by using the statement GRANT
  <privilege> .... TO SHARE on the database
  samples, the schema finance, or the concrete table
  stocks_share to the consumer account locator
  <consumer _account>.

- We checked privileges using SHOW GRANTS TO SHARE
  <share_name>. See Figure 10-4.

created_on	privilege	granted_on	name	granted_to	grantee_name	grant_option	granted_by
2019-07-17 ...	USAGE	DATABASE	SAMPLES	SHARE	⟨꙳⟩꙳꙳꙳ꙮꙮ.STOCKS_SHARE	false	SYSADMIN
2019-07-17 ...	USAGE	SCHEMA	SAMPLES.FINANCE	SHARE	⟨꙳⟩꙳꙳꙳ꙮꙮ.STOCKS_SHARE	false	SYSADMIN
2019-07-17 ...	SELECT	TABLE	SAMPLES.FINANCE.STOCKS_DATA	SHARE	⟨꙳⟩꙳꙳꙳ꙮꙮ.STOCKS_SHARE	false	SYSADMIN

Figure 10-4. *Grants on a share object*

- We added a new account to a share using ALTER
  SHARE <share_name> ADD ACCOUNTS=<consumer
  _account>;.

3. Log into your consumer account called <consumer_
   account>. Check access to the table via the consumer
   account.

4. Switch to the Worksheets tab and execute SQL. See Figure 10-5.

   Now see Listing 10-3.

Listing 10-3. Showing the Available Share

```
use role accountadmin;
show shares;
desc share <consumer_account>.STOCKS_SHARE;
```

Row	created_on	kind	name	database_name
1	2019-09-29 23...	INBOUND	▩▩▩▩.STOCKS_SHARE	SHARED_DB
2	2018-08-15 08:...	INBOUND	SNOWFLAKE.ACCOUNT_USAGE	SNOWFLAKE

Figure 10-5. *Available shares in consumer account*

5. Let's create a database based on the share. See Figure 10-6.

   ```
   create database shared_db from share <provider_
   account>.STOCKS_SHARE;
   ```

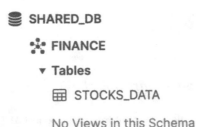

SHARED_DB

FINANCE

▼ Tables

STOCKS_DATA

No Views in this Schema

Figure 10-6. *Available shared objects in the consumer account*

6.   Query the shared table. See Figure 10-7.

```
9  select * from SHARED_DB.Finance.STOCKS_DATA;
```

Results   Data Preview

✔ Query ID   SQL   433ms   6 rows

Row	ID	SYMBOL	DATE	TIME	BID_PRICE	ASK_PRICE
1	1	TDC	2019-09-28	10:15:00	36.3	36
2	2	TDC	2019-07-29	11:14:00	36.5	36.2
3	3	ORCL	2019-09-28	11:15:00	57.8	59.9
4	4	ORCL	2019-07-29	09:11:00	57.3	57.9

Figure 10-7. *Querying the shared table*

Data Sharing Using a Secure View

If you have a table, you need to perform these steps to organize access to
the table:

1.   Add a new column to a table to divide data into a
     few groups.

2.   Create a mapping table (mapping the name of the
     groups and the name of the Snowflake account).

3.   Create a secure view on a table.

4. Create a share object.

5. Add the secure view name to the share and grant privileges.

6. Add the account to the share object.

Let's do an example.

SHARING A TABLE USING SECURE VIEW

Let's look at how to provide access row-level sharing using a secure view.

1. Log into your Snowflake account.

2. Switch to a worksheet and execute the code in Listing 10-4.

Listing 10-4. Modifying the Table and Adding Values for Grouping Data

```
use role sysadmin;
alter table samples.finance.stocks_data
  add column access_id string;

update finance.stocks_data
    set access_id = 'GRP_1'
where id in (1,2,3,4);

update finance.stocks_data
    set access_id = 'GRP_2'
where id in (5,6);
commit;
  select * from samples.finance.stocks_data;
```

In Listing 10-4, we did the following:

- We changed the table from the previous example by adding a new column called access_id.

- We divided the stock data into two groups.

  - IT companies: GRP_1

  - Auto companies: GRP_2

Figure 10-8 shows some summary data of the table.

ROWID	SYMBOL	DATE	TIME	BID_PRICE	ASK_PRICE	BID_CNT	ASK_CNT	ACCESS_ID
1	TDC	2019-07-18	10:15:00	36.3	36	10	10	GRP_1
2	TDC	2019-05-19	11:14:00	36.5	36.2	10	10	GRP_1
3	ORCL	2019-07-18	11:15:00	57.8	59.9	13	13	GRP_1
4	ORCL	2019-05-19	09:11:00	57.3	57.9	12	12	GRP_1
5	TSLA	2019-07-18	11:01:00	255.2	256.4	22	22	GRP_2
6	TSLA	2019-05-19	11:13:00	255.2	255.7	23	23	GRP_2

Figure 10-8. *Table with column for grouping data*

3. To provide public access based on a secure view, execute the code in Listing 10-5.

Listing 10-5. Creating a Mapping Table

```
use role sysadmin;
create or replace table samples.finance.access_map (
  access_id string,
  account string
);

# add access to tech companies for my account
insert into samples.finance.access_map values('GRP_1',
current_account());
```

```
# add access to tech companies for my account
insert into samples.finance.access_map values('GRP_2',
'<consumer_account>');
commit;
select * from samples.finance.access_map;
```

In Listing 10-5, we did the following:

- We created a mapping table called access_map;.

- We filled the table with values:

    - Group #1 of stocks for our account

    - Group #2 of stocks for <consumer_account>

4. To provide public access based on a secure view, execute the
   code in Listing 10-6.

Listing 10-6. Creating the Secure View on the Table

```
create or replace schema samples.public;
create or replace secure view samples.public.stocks as
    select sd.symbol, sd.date, sd.time, sd.bid_price,
    sd.ask_price, sd.bid_cnt, sd.ask_cnt
    from samples.finance.stocks_data sd
    join samples.finance.access_map  am on sd.access_id =
    am.access_id
    and am.account = current_account();
grant select on samples.public.stocks  to public;
```

In Listing 10-6, we did the following:

- We created a new public schema.

- We created a secure view called samples.public.
  stocks; based on the table and the mapping table.

- We used the function current_account() for dynamically identifying the user account.

- We granted privileges to access the secure view.

5. We tested the access to the table and the secure view.

Now see Listing 10-7.

Listing 10-7. Checking Access to Tables

```
select count(*) from samples.finance.stocks_data;
select * from samples.finance.stocks_data;
select count(*) from samples.public.stocks;
select * from samples.public.stocks;
select * from samples.public.stocks
where symbol = 'TDC';
```

6. Test the access to the table and secure view by using the session parameter simulated_data_sharing_consumer. See Figure 10-9.

Now see Listing 10-8.

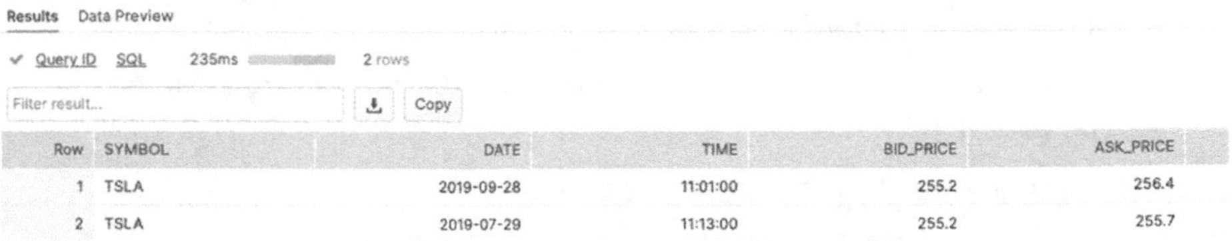

Results Data Preview

✓ Query ID SQL 235ms ▬▬▬▬ 2 rows

Filter result... [⬇] [Copy]

Row	SYMBOL	DATE	TIME	BID_PRICE	ASK_PRICE
1	TSLA	2019-09-28	11:01:00	255.2	256.4
2	TSLA	2019-07-29	11:13:00	255.2	255.7

Figure 10-9. *The data of the secure view available to the consumer (in session simulated mode)*

Listing 10-8. Checking Access to the Table Using a Session Parameter

```
alter session set simulated_data_sharing_consumer=<consumer_name>;
select * from samples.public.stocks;
```

7. Create a share object, add the secure view to the share, and grant privileges.

Now see Listing 10-9.

Listing 10-9. Adding the Secure View in the Share Object and Grant Privileges

```
alter session set simulated_data_sharing_consumer='<provider_
account>';
use role accountadmin;
create or replace share share_sv;
grant usage on database samples to share share_sv;
grant usage on schema samples.public to share share_sv;
grant select on samples.public.stocks to share share_sv;
show grants to share share_sv;
alter share share_sv set accounts = <consumer_accounts>;
show shares;
```

In Listing 10-9, we did the following:

- We turned back to the session of the producer account.

- We created a new share object called share_sv.

- We added the secure view to the share.

- We granted privileges to access the secure view for the consumer account.

8. Execute the script in Listing 10-10 on the consumer side. See Figure 10-10.

Figure 10-10. *The view available for the consumer*

Listing 10-10. Consumer's Script

```
use role accountadmin;

show shares;
create database shared_views_db from share <provider_
account>.share_sv;
grant imported privileges on database shared_views_db to
sysadmin;
use role sysadmin;
show views;
use warehouse <warehouse_name>;
select * from stocks;
```

In Listing 10-10, we did the following:

- We created a database from the share object called share_sv.

- We granted imported privileges from the share object to the sysadmin user.

- We got access to the secure view called stocks.

Figure 10-11. *The data of the secure view available to the consumer*

Summary

In this chapter, we covered the Snowflake data sharing feature that provides an easy, fast, and secure way to distribute data. Moreover, you learned about share objects and considered several basic options for using these features.

Finally, we walked through two examples: a simple way to share a table and an advanced way to share one by using a secure view.

In the next chapter, you will learn about how to design modern analytical solutions based on Snowflake services.

CHAPTER 11

Designing a Modern Analytics Solution with Snowflake

You are now familiar with the Snowflake data warehouse (DW) and its advantages over other DW solutions. However, a typical organization won't be using Snowflake alone. Snowflake is part of an analytics solution that consists of multiple components, including business intelligence and data integration tools.

In this chapter, you will learn about a modern solution architecture and the role of Snowflake in it. We will cover the following topics:

- Modern analytics solution architecture

- Snowflake partner ecosystem

- Integration with Matillion ETL and Tableau

This chapter will help you to learn how to build an end-to-end solution using leading cloud tools for business intelligence and data integration. You will launch Matillion ETL and load data into the Snowflake DW. In addition, you will connect to Tableau Desktop and build dashboards.

© Dmitry Anoshin, Dmitry Shirokov, Donna Strok 2020
D. Anoshin et al., *Jumpstart Snowflake*, https://doi.org/10.1007/978-1-4842-5328-1_11

Modern Analytics Solution Architecture

Nowadays, every organization wants to be data-driven to generate more value for customers and stakeholders. The organization's management understands the value of data and treats it as an asset. They are ready to invest in modern cloud solutions like Snowflake that are scalable and secure. However, Snowflake is just one part of the analytical ecosystem. It is the core data storage for all organization data, and it provides robust access to the data.

You need more elements in order to build the right solution. These elements include data integration tools, business intelligence, and data modeling tools. Figure 11-1 highlights the key elements of a modern analytics solution.

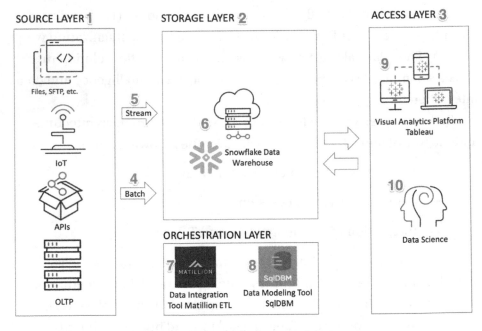

Figure 11-1. *Modern analytics solution architecture*

Figure 11-1 gives you an idea of how a typical analytics solution can look. I've already added Matillion ETL and Tableau to the diagram because we are going to use them in this chapter. However, you have a choice to use other products as well.

Table 11-1 describes additional information for each element of the architecture.

Table 11-1. *Key Elements of Architecture Diagram*

Element	Description
Source layer	The source layer includes all the data sources available at your organization. This could include transactional databases, files, NoSQL databases, business applications, external APIs, sensors, and IoT.
Storage layer	The storage layer is the core of solution. You may hear about data platforms, data lakes, and data warehouses. This is the place for all of them. You are ingesting data into the storage layer from the source layers, and you store this data for further analysis, data discovery, or the decision-making process.
Access layer	The access layer is nontechnical. The main goal is to provide access for business users and allow them to interact with data through BI and SQL.
Stream	Streaming is a method of data ingesting using real-time data injection. For example, you can collect data from sensors, and you have a strict SLA to analyze the data and make decisions.
Batch	Batch Processing is a method of data ingesting. For example, for DWs, we load data once per day. Sometimes, we should load data more frequently.
Snowflake	Snowflake is cloud data warehouse that can serve as a data lake. It can collect data from both batching and streaming pipelines.

(continued)

Table 11-1. (*continued*)

Element	Description
Matillion ETL	Matillion ETL is a cloud-native tool that is responsible for the extract, load, and transform (ELT) process. It was built for the cloud and provides a visual interface for building data pipelines. The ELT tool is responsible for all data movement and data transformation.
SqlDBM	SqlDBM is a cloud data modeling tool. It was the first cloud tool that was built for Snowflake. Without a proper data model, you can't deliver a quality DW. Moreover, it helps to communicate with business stakeholders and collaborate with a team.
Tableau	Tableau is a visual analytics platform that connects to Snowflake and provides access for the business users and helps them slice/dice data and deliver insights. In other words, it is business intelligence tool.
Data science tools	Data science tools provide advanced analytics capabilities. It could be an open source product, programming language (R/Python), or enterprise solution like Spark Databricks.

In this chapter, we will show how to build simple solutions using Matillion ETL, Snowflake, and Tableau. We won't spend much time on setting up a real source system and will use sample data sets that we will load into Snowflake with Matillion and then visualize with Tableau. Moreover, we won't build a streaming solution or talk about lambda architecture. Based on our experience in 80 percent of use cases, using a data warehouse, business intelligence, and ELT is sufficient for a typical organization.

Snowflake Partner Ecosystem

Snowflake has many technology partners, and it provides good integration with them. In addition, it has a convenient feature called Partner Connect that allows you to launch a solution via the Snowflake web interface, as shown in Figure 11-2.

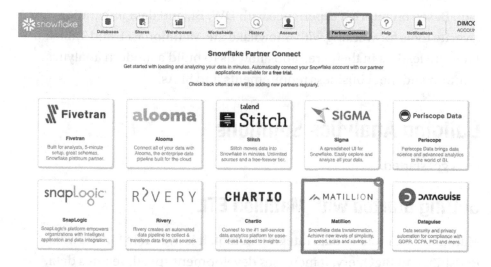

Figure 11-2. *Snowflake Partner Connect page*

Moreover, Snowflake provides native drivers like JDBC, ODBC, and others for connecting to third-party tools such as Tableau, SqlDBM, Spark, and others. Figure 11-3 shows the list of available drivers. You can click Help ➤ Download to get to this menu.

Figure 11-3. *Snowflake drivers*

For our solution, we should choose a data integration tool and BI tool. Based on our rich experience with DW, BI, and data integration, our favorite tools for working with Snowflake are Matillion ETL and Tableau. They are leaders in their area and allow us to build a modern analytics solution and meet business requirements and SLAs.

Building Analytics Solutions

Let's get started.

Getting Started with Matillion ETL

Matillion ETL is cloud data integration tool. It is available for Snowflake, Redshift, and BigQuery. It increases development speed, secures data, provides rich data transformation functionality, and offers many prebuilt data connectors for Salesforce, Mailchimp, Facebook, and others. One of the biggest advantages of the tool is that it looks and feels like a traditional ETL tool with a friendly user interface where developers can drag and drop components to build their data pipeline.

To start with Matillion ETL, click the Matillion box in Figure 11-1. This will open a new window and ask permission to create objects within a Snowflake account. You can see the list of objects in Table 11-2.

***Table 11-2.** List of Matillion Objects*

Object	Object
Database	PC_MATILLION_DB
Warehouse	PC_MATILLION_WH (X-Small)
Role	PC_MATILLION_ROLE
Username	Snowflake-snowflake

After activation, the tool will immediately transfer you to the Matillion ETL web interface. This is connected to your Snowflake cluster, and you may start to work immediately. This increases your time to market.

Let's load some initial data into Snowflake using Matillion.

Note   Our Snowflake cluster is hosted on AWS. When we launched a Matillion ETL instance from the Partner Connect page, we created the EC2 instance with Matillion ETL. It was created in a different AWS account. We can launch Matillion ETL in our AWS account by finding it in the AWS Marketplace. In this case, we will get full control over the Matillion ETL instance, connect via SSH, use an application load balancer, adjust security groups, and so on.

RUNNING OUR FIRST JOB WITH MATILLION ETL

We will use a demo Matillion ETL job and sample airport data in order to create our first ELT job and then load and transform data for our Snowflake DW. Let's get started.

1. Log into Matillion ETL. You can use the URL, password, and username that you've received in the Matillion activation e-mail.

2. Navigate to Partner Connect Group ➤ Snowflake Project. You will find two demo jobs, called dim_airport_setup and dim_airports.

3. Open the dim_airport_setup job by clicking it twice. In Figure 11-4, we are showing key elements of the Matillion web interface.

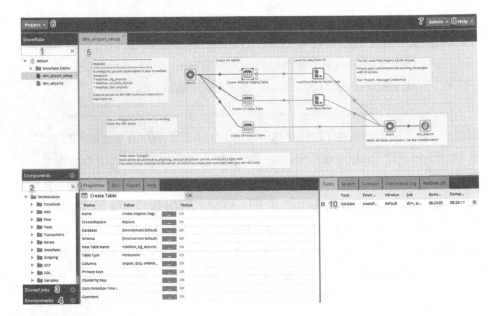

Figure 11-4. *Modern analytics solution architecture*

When you are working with Matillion, you are working mostly from a browser. The same is true for Snowflake. Table 11-3 describes the key elements of the Matillion ETL web interface shown in Figure 11-4.

Table 11-3. *Key Elements of Matillion ETL Web Interface*

Element in Figure 11-4	Description
1	The job list pane includes all the jobs that you are building for this project. Moreover, you can organize jobs with folders. There are two types of jobs. A *transformation* job (green) is responsible for data transformation inside Snowflake. An *orchestration* job (blue) is responsible for extracting and loading data from/to external sources.
2	The Components pane includes all the components available for this job type (blue or green). You can easily drag and drop components and build pipelines.
3	The "Shared job" pane lists the shared jobs. A shared job is a kind of aggregated job. For example, you can build a new job and reuse it as a single component.
4	The Environments pane lists the environments. For example, by default we have one environment that is connected to our Snowflake cluster. If we want to load data into a different Snowflake cluster or from another AWS account, we should create a new environment and specify the credentials.
5	Canvas is our development environment where we can drag and drop components from the Components pane or "Shared job" pane and organize them into the data pipeline. Moreover, we can add notes with tips and documentation.
6	The Project menu is the main menu for Matillion ETL, where you can manage existing projects, switch to others, and manage variables, schedules, API profiles, and many others.
7	The Admin menu is available for the Matillion administrator. From this menu you can manage Matillion users, manage backups, and download logs.

(continued)

Table 11-3. (*continued*)

Element in Figure 11-4	Description
8	The Help menu allows you to get support information, manage active sessions, and manage license keys.
9	Component options connect you to Snowflake and provide access to business users and help them slice/dice data and deliver insights. In other words, this is a business intelligence tool.
10	The Status menu provides information about currently running tasks, shows the command log, and displays notices about available updates.

You have learned about the key elements of the Matillion web interface, so you can now run a job. Click the right button on the canvas and choose "Run job (snowflake)." Matillion will run the current job using the environment name *snowflake*. This job consists of multiple steps.

    a. Create tables using the Create Table component.

    b. Load data from S3 into the staging tables using the S3 Load component.

    c. Execute the transformation job `dim_airport` that will transform raw semistructured data into a tabular format and load it into a dimension table.

Note   During this exercise, we loaded the Matillion sample data set that is stored in an Amazon S3 bucket of Matillion. This bucket is public and is available to everyone. If you have Snowflake on Azure, then you will load data from Blob Storage.

---

4. After the job is finished, we can go back to the Snowflake web
    UI and check the new objects that were created by Matillion.
    Figure 11-5 shows the list of Snowflake tables that were
    created by the Matillion orchestration job.

Table Name	Schema	Creation Time ▾	Owner	Rows	Size	Comment
matillion_us_state_lookup	PUBLIC	7:39:28 PM	PC_MATILLION_RO...	|50	|1.5KB	
matillion_dim_airports	PUBLIC	7:39:28 PM	PC_MATILLION_RO...	3.4K	101KB	
matillion_stg_airports	PUBLIC	7:39:27 PM	PC_MATILLION_RO...	3.4K	137.5KB	

Figure 11-5. *Snowflake tables created by Matillion ETL*

We launched Matillion ETL and loaded sample data into the Snowflake DW. In
a real-world scenario, we would create many more jobs and collect data from
external sources. For example, for marketing analytics use cases, we need to
load data from social media platforms such as Facebook, Twitter, YouTube, and
so on. Matillion ETL provides prebuilt connectors that will save time for data
engineers or ETL developers.

Moreover, for a quality solution, we should design a data model for querying
our data. We might choose a technique like using Data Vault, dimensional
modeling, and so on. The best choice for the Snowflake data model is SqlDBM.

The final step is to connect to a BI tool. We need a BI tool for simplifying
access for nontechnical users. With Tableau, business users can do data
discovery using drag-and-drop methods and powerful analytics and
visualization capabilities. For our sample solution, we will install Tableau
Desktop and connect to the `matillion_dim_airport` table in order to
visualize data.

Getting Started with Tableau

Tableau is a leading visual analytics platform. There are many tools available on the market, but Tableau stands out among them. We have worked with many different tools from leading vendors and found that Tableau is the most powerful tool for business intelligence and self-service. Moreover, it has a large and friendly community. If you have never worked with Tableau, now is a good time to try it. Connecting Tableau to Snowflake allows us to use best-of-breed technologies working together. Tableau is available in Server and Desktop versions. Moreover, it has a mobile application. Let's get Tableau and connect to the Snowflake cluster.

BUILDING OUR FIRST VISUALIZATION WITH TABLEAU AND SNOWFLAKE

During this exercise, we will install Tableau Desktop and connect it to the Snowflake DW. Then we will visualize the `matillion_airport_dim` data.

1. Let's download and install Tableau Desktop. Go to `https://www.tableau.com/products/desktop/download` and download a recent version of Tableau Desktop. It is available for macOS and Windows. Then install it.

2. Open Tableau Desktop and connect to Snowflake, as shown in Figure 11-6.

Figure 11-6. *Tableau Desktop connection to Snowflake*

Note   To connect to the Snowflake DW, you need to download the ODBC driver from the Snowflake web UI. Select Help ➤ Download ➤ ODBC driver. Download it and install.

---

3. Then, you should enter your credentials in order to connect to Snowflake from Tableau. You can use the Matillion credentials that were created during the Matillion ETL initializing, including the user role, or you can use your master credentials. You should use your admin Snowflake credentials. Figure 11-7 shows an example of the connection options.

Snowflake

Server: `<your host>.snowflakecomputing.com`

Role: Optional

Enter information to sign in to the server:

Authentication: Username and Password

Username: `<your user name>`

Password: ••••••••••|

SAML IdP(Okta):

Initial SQL...   Sign In

Figure 11-7. *Snowflake connection window*

4. Click Sign In and then enter the following:

   a. Warehouse: PC_MATILLION_WH

   b. Database: PC_MATILLION_DB

   c. Schema: Public

   Then drag and drop the matillion_dim_airports table to the connection canvas.

5. Click Sheet 1, and you will jump into the development area. You just created your first Tableau live data source.

Note   The Tableau data source supports live and extract options. Extract will query all data from the data source and cache it into an internal columnar data store called Hyper. The live connection will query data from the data source on demand. This is the right strategy for a big volume of data. With a live connection, Snowflake will do the heavy lifting, and Tableau will render the result. This is the secret to doing big data analytics.

6. Let's create a quick visualization using the available data. Say we want to know the number of airports across states and order them in descending order. In Figure 11-8 you can see the Tableau Desktop interface and a simple report.

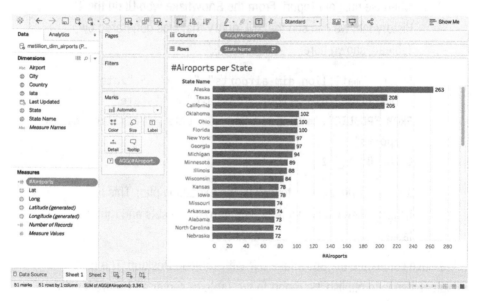

Figure 11-8.   *Number of airports in Alaska*

Did you know that Alaska has the most airports of all states? This is good insight. We built this report by dragging and dropping the dimension (blue) State Name into the Rows pane and Calculated Field #Airports into the Columns pane. To create a calculated field, click the right button in the Measures pane and choose Create Calculated Field. Then use the following syntax:

```
COUNTD([Airport])
```

This count the distinct (unique) number of airports names. We will put a measure also in the Label pane to provide a label for each bar.

7. It is interesting to look at Snowflake to see what was happening when we built our report. From the Snowflake web UI on the History tab, we can see the SQL query that was generated by Tableau, shown here:

```
SELECT "matillion_dim_airports"."iata" AS "iata",
  "matillion_dim_airports"."state" AS "state"
FROM "PUBLIC"."matillion_dim_airports" "matillion_dim_
airports"
GROUP BY 1,  2
```

Moreover, we are able to look at the execution plan. This is helpful when we are working with large data sets and multiple tables.

We have connected the Snowflake DW with Tableau Desktop. The next logical step is to publish the report to the Tableau server and share it with stakeholders.

> **Note**   With Tableau, you can leverage the unique features of
> Snowflake such as querying and visualizing semistructured data,
> working with the Time Travel feature, sharing data, implementing
> role-based security, and using custom aggregation. Moreover,
> we can integrate Tableau and Matillion. You can find more good
> information about this at `https://rockyourdata.cloud/best-`
> `practices-matillion-etl-and-tableau/`.

Summary

In this chapter, we covered the Snowflake partner ecosystem, and you
learned about a modern analytics architecture and its key elements.
Moreover, we connected to the best cloud ELT tool for Snowflake, which
is Matillion ETL, and ran our first job. Then, we built a report with the best
visual analytics tool, called Tableau. At the end of this chapter, we created
analytics solution that can be scaled and is ready for use in production.
Using this example, you can build your analytics solution and get
immediate value.

In the next chapter, we will talk about some data use cases for
Snowflake. You will learn how Snowflake can handle a large volume of data.

CHAPTER 12

Snowflake and Data Science

"You're only given a little spark of madness. You mustn't lose it."

—Robin Williams,
"Little spark of madness" stand-up, 1977

Nowadays, data is one of the main assets of any company. As a result, each team of analysts is faced with the need to organize data science processes. Snowflake is a smart choice as a data source for storing structured and semistructured data.

In other words, elastic storage and computes allow you to store an unlimited amount of data at no extra cost with the ability to search for insights through data analysis and model building.

Additionally, the platform has integration possibilities with the most popular data analytical solutions.

In this chapter, you will learn about how Snowflake and data science platforms work together. We will cover the following topics:

- Snowflake-supported advanced analytics solutions

- Apache Spark introduction

- Snowflake and Spark connector

- Snowflake and Databricks

© Dmitry Anoshin, Dmitry Shirokov, Donna Strok 2020
D. Anoshin et al., *Jumpstart Snowflake*, https://doi.org/10.1007/978-1-4842-5328-1_12

Snowflake and the Analytics Ecosystem

Snowflake supports many popular analytical solutions. Table 12-1 shows some of the platforms that are integrated with Snowflake.

Table 12-1. *Popular Analytics Solutions That Work with Snowflake*

Tool	Description
Alteryx	Alteryx[1] is a self-service data analytics platform.
Apache Spark	Apache Spark[2] is an open source cluster computing framework.
Databricks	Databricks[3] is a cloud-based big data processing company founded by the creators of Apache Spark.
DataRobot	DataRobot[4] is a predictive analytics platform to rapidly build and deploy predictive models in the cloud or in an enterprise.
H2O.io	H2O.io[5] is an open source machine learning and artificial intelligence platform.
R Studio	R Studio[6] is an open source integrated development environment for R.
Qubola	Qubola[7] is cloud-native data platform based on Apache Spark, Apache Airflow, and Presto.

---

[1]You can find more information about the Alteryx platform at `https://www.alteryx.com/`.

[2]You can find more information about Apache Spark at `https://spark.apache.org/`.

[3]You can find more information about the Databricks platform at `https://databricks.com/`.

[4]You can find more information about DataRobot at `https://www.datarobot.com/`.

[5]You can find more information about the H2O platform at `https://www.h2o.ai/`.

[6]You can find more information about R Studio at `https://www.rstudio.com/`.

[7]You can find more information about Qubola at `https://www.qubole.com/`.

Snowflake and Apache Spark

Let's look at an example of how the interaction between the database and the analytical platform works. Apache Spark is the de facto industry standard for big data engineering and analytics. Spark is an open source analytics framework based on a distributed computing cluster. It usually uses engineering data pipelines, including streaming mode, ad hoc analysis, machine learning, graph analysis, and other types of analytics.

Machine learning is becoming increasingly popular in many companies because it can significantly impact many of the company's business processes. Spark can work for model training and production. We can build a machine learning model using Spark MLlib, which is an internal machine learning library using distributed, highly scaling algorithms. Additionally, Spark works well with Pandas,[8] Scikit-learn,[9] TensorFlow,[10] and other popular statistical, machine learning, and deep learning libraries.

Moreover, you can use Apache MLflow[11] for organizing the lifecycle of the model and Apache Airflow[12] or similar solutions for building data pipelines.

---

[8]Pandas is a Python library providing data structures and data analysis methods. For more information, see `https://pandas.pydata.org`.

[9]Scikit-learn is a free Python machine learning library. For more information, see `https://scikit-learn.org`.

[10]TensorFlow is an open source deep learning library. For more information, see `https://www.tensorflow.org`.

[11]MLflow is an open source platform for the machine learning lifecycle. For more information, see `https://mlflow.org/`.

[12]Apache Airflow is a schedule and monitor workflows tool. For more information, see `https://airflow.apache.org`.

Data scientists and analysts prefer to use SQL, R, and Python. Data engineers usually use languages such as Python, Java, and Scala. Spark provides an API with a different number of languages, including all these languages. It depends on the assets and knowledge base of your team members; each can be writing Spark code that executes on a distributed cluster of machines. Your company can choose the optimal strategy for deployment because Apache Spark can be set up and deployed on-premises or in the cloud. Most popular cloud providers such as Amazon AWS, Microsoft Azure, and Google supply Spark as a component or service. AWS supports Spark as part of an EMR[13] service. Microsoft supports Spark in the Azure Hadoop–based HDInsight[14] as well as the Azure Databricks platform. Additionally, Google Cloud Dataproc[15] is a managed service based on Hadoop with Spark.

Let's look at the main components of Apache Spark; see Figure 12-1.

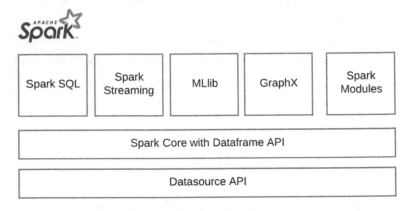

Figure 12-1. *Apache Spark high-level components*

---

[13]AWS Elastic MapReduce (EMR) is a Hadoop managed service on AWS. For more information, see `https://aws.amazon.com/emr/`.

[14]HDInsight is a Hadoop-managed service on Azure. For more information, see `https://azure.microsoft.com/en-us/services/hdinsight/`.

[15]Google Cloud Dataproc is a Hadoop-managed service on GCP. For more information, see `https://cloud.google.com/dataproc/`.

Table 12-2 describes the components of the platform.

Table 12-2. *Components of Apache Spark*

Component	Description
Spark SQL	Spark SQL is the module for working with structured data by using SQL. It is compliant with the SQL ANSI 2011 specification and also supports Hive QL.
Spark Streaming	Spark Streaming is a Spark Structured Streaming API that allows you to build a scalable data pipeline solution that works in near-real-time mode.
MLlib	MLlib is the implementation of machine learning algorithms in a scalable and distributed manner.
GraphX	GraphX is the module for graph analytics. For instance, you can use graph analysis as part of the implementation of fraud analytics or customer churn analysis.
Spark Core with Dataframe API	Spark Core is the distributed scalable engine that deploys on different types of big data clusters such as Mesos, Hadoop YARN, and Kubernetes. It provides a high-level abstraction including RDD and Dataframe[16] for operating with structured and semi/unstructured data by using the Python, R, and Scala/Java languages.
Datasource API	The Datasource API provides the ability to deelop connectors for connecting to Apache Spark. Snowflake has already developed such a library.
Spark Modules	Spark has an ecosystem for the development and distribution of Spark-compatible libraries.

---

[16]Spark provides data frames and data sets. For more information, see
https://spark.apache.org/docs/latest/sql-programming-guide.html.

Connector for Apache Spark

Snowflake provides Apache Spark Connector,[17] which allows you to use Snowflake and Spark together. Let's dive into how it works.

Figure 12-2 shows a data flow process between Snowflake data warehouse services and managed Apache Spark.

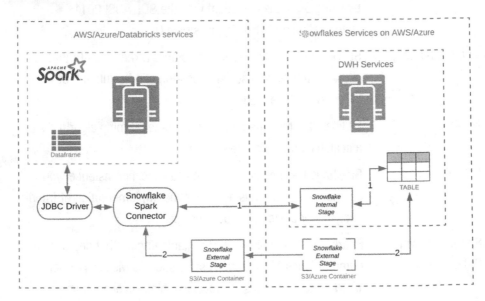

Figure 12-2. *Bidirectional data transfer between Snowflake and Spark*

The connector supports two modes of data transfer, depending on whether the internal stage is used or external. Stages can be based on an AWS S3 or Azure Blob Storage container. Internal stages automatically create and drop during data transfer inside the Snowflake session. However, you can choose the external stages if you prefer to manage the data transfer yourself.

---

[17]For more information about Snowflake Connector for Spark, see `https://docs.snowflake.net/manuals/user-guide/spark-connector.html`.

Note Best practice is to use internal transfer. Use external transfer only if there is a need to store data for more than 36 hours.

Additionally, one of the key features of the Spark connector is query pushdown optimization. *Pushdown optimization* is an approach in which the logic for transforming or querying data happens on the database side. The adapter has deep integration with Spark and will be able to read Spark's logical query plans and transfer fully or partially executed to Snowflake. This allows you to reduce the amount of data being moved between the Snowflake database and Spark, which dramatically improves performance. See Table 12-3.

Table 12-3. *Interaction Between Spark and Snowflake*

Interaction	Description
Spark dataframe	A Spark dataframe is the data structure in the distributed memory of Apache Spark that can be automatically created and based on the data from Snowflake's table. The schema of the table and the dataframe schema must match. Otherwise, you must specify the mapping.[18] In the opposite direction, it is the data structure that stores the data that is written to the table.
Snowflake JDBC driver	The Snowflake JDBC driver is a high-performance optimized driver developed by the Snowflake corporation.

(continued)

---

[18]For more information about column mapping, see `https://docs.snowflake.net/manuals/user-guide/spark-connector-use.html#label-spark-options`.

Table 12-3. (*continued*)

Interaction	Description
Snowflake Spark Connector	Snowflake Spark Connector is a connector that implements the Spark Datasource API for Snowflake and is published as the Maven[19] package.
Snowflake internal/ external stages	Snowflake internal/external stages are Snowflake stages used by the data transfer process.
Snowflake table	A Snowflake table is the source/target table into the Snowflake DB.

Working with Databricks

Databricks provides the Databricks Unified Analytics Platform,[20] which is a data science and data engineering platform with tools for data engineers to build data pipelines, for data scientists to build machine learning models, and for business users to consume real-time dashboards.

In addition to the Spark engine, the platform provides many additional enterprise-level components for building a complete process for gathering insights from data sets, as well as designing and testing machine learning models.

---

[19]Maven is a build automation tool used primarily for Java projects. For more information, see https://maven.apache.org/.

[20]For more information, see https://databricks.com/product/ unified-analytics-platform.

Databricks has already set up Snowflake Spark Connector. We can easily use the interface for quickly setting up a connection between data platforms. See Figure 12-3 and Table 12-4.

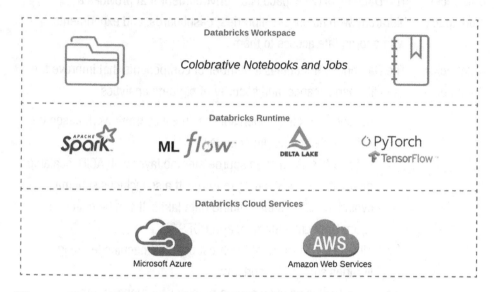

Figure 12-3. *Elements of Databricks Unified Analytics Platform*

Table 12-4. *Components of Databricks Unified Analytics Platform*

Component	Description
Databricks Workspace	The Databricks Workspace is an environment that provides a hierarchy with notebooks, libraries, dashboards, and experiments with appropriate access to them.

Databricks Runtime	The Databricks Runtime is a number of components that improve the usability, performance, and security of big data analytics.
	
	 • Apache Spark is an open source analytics framework based on a distributed computing cluster.
	 • Delta Lake[21] is an open source storage layer with ACID, scalable metadata, and versioning features. It also includes schema evolution features for building data lakes. It can be built on S3, Azure Data Lake Storage, and HDFS.[22]
	 • ML Libraries is a list of the most popular machine learning libraries such as TensorFlow.
	 • ML Flow[23] is an open source platform for managing the machine learning lifecycle, including the following:
	     • ML Flow Project provides a code packaging format.
	     • ML Flow Models provides a model packaging format. You can deploy it to Docker or Azure ML for serving Apache Spark.
	     • ML Flow Tracking is a component for tracking experiments, including code, parameters, and metrics.

Databricks Cloud Services	The platform can be deployed on AWS and Azure. Databricks is software as a service. This means the platform provides the benefits of a fully managed service and reduces infrastructure complexity.

---

[21]For more information about Delta Lake, see `https://delta.io/`.

[22]For more information about Apache Hadoop Distributed File System, see `https://hadoop.apache.org/`.

[23]For more information about MLFlow, see `https://mlflow.org/`.

USING SNOWFLAKE AND DATABRICKS TOGETHER

Let's see how the Databricks interface works with Snowflake. This is just an example of how you might do this.

1. Sign into Azure at `azure.microsoft.com`.[24]

Note   The minimum requirement for a Databricks cluster is two nodes. Your Azure account has to be "pay as you go." Please check your account's limits and quotas[25] and pricing details.[26]

---

2. Log into your Azure account.

3. Create a new Databricks service using Home ➤ Azure Databricks ➤ Create Azure Databricks service. See Figure 12-4.

---

[24]For more information about Microsoft Azure, see `https://azure.microsoft.com`.

[25]For more information about limits, see `https://docs.microsoft.com/en-us/azure/azure-subscription-service-limits`.

[26]For more information about Azure Databricks, see `https://azure.microsoft.com/en-us/pricing/details/databricks/`.

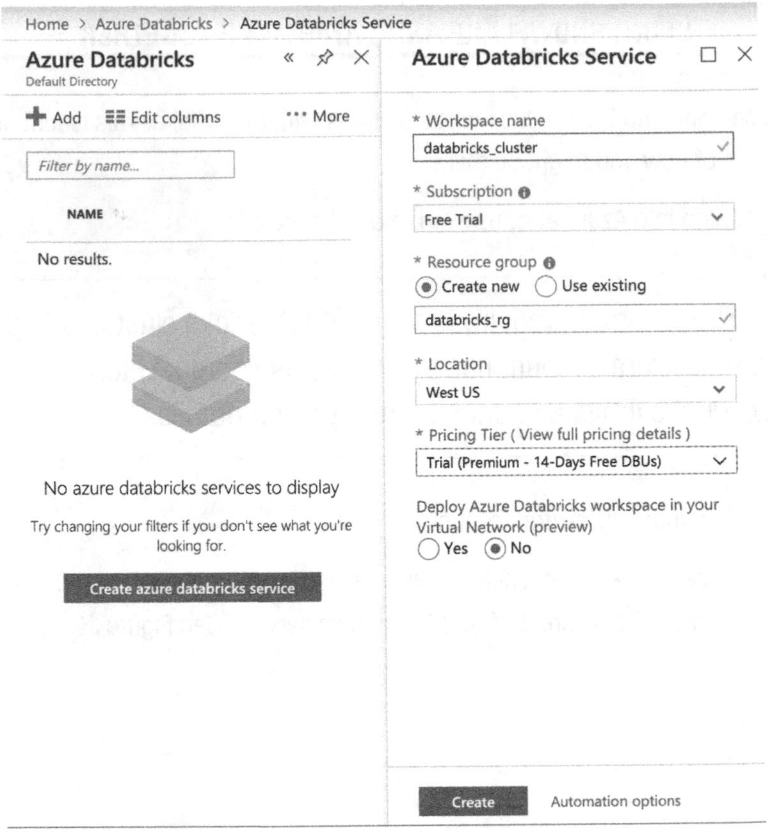

Figure 12-4. *Creating a new Azure Databricks service*

4. Open a Databricks environment.

A Databricks notebook practically represents an extended version of Python Notebook. See Figure 12-5.

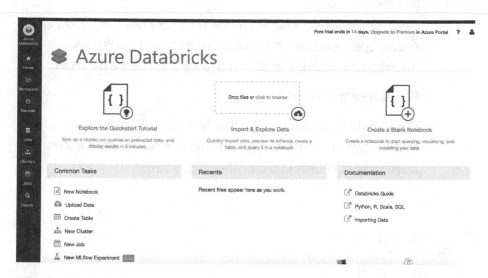

Figure 12-5. *Azure Databricks environment*

5. Create a new small Spark cluster by selecting Cluster ➤ Create cluster. See Figure 12-6.

Figure 12-6. *Launching a new Spark cluster*

Set Cluster Name to *db_cluster*.

Databricks Runtime 5.3 ML means the set of core runtimes, including Apache Spark and Scala; machine learning libraries like Pandas, PyTorch, and TensorFlow; and other popular data science packages.

Next, use Python version 3.

Finally, we have to choose the Worker Type setup. We can use the standard type here. For better performance, we can choose a worker called Databricks Delta Caching.[27] See Figure 12-7.

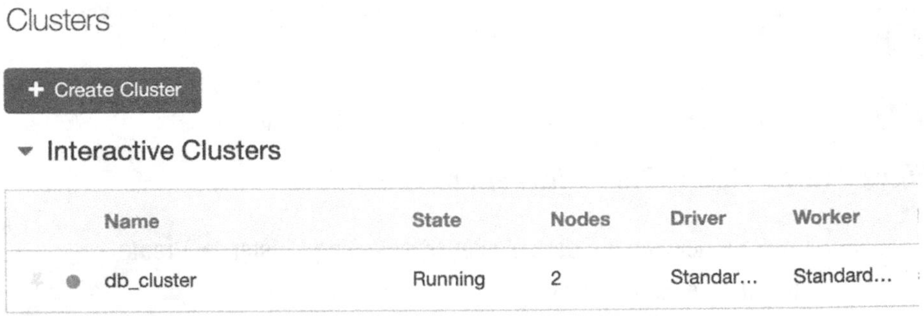

Clusters

+ Create Cluster

▾ Interactive Clusters

	Name	State	Nodes	Driver	Worker	
●	db_cluster	Running	2	Standar...	Standard...	

Figure 12-7. *Launching a new Spark cluster*

6. Create a new notebook using Azure Databricks ➤ Create a blank notebook, call it snowflake_test, and attach the existing cluster. See Figure 12-8.

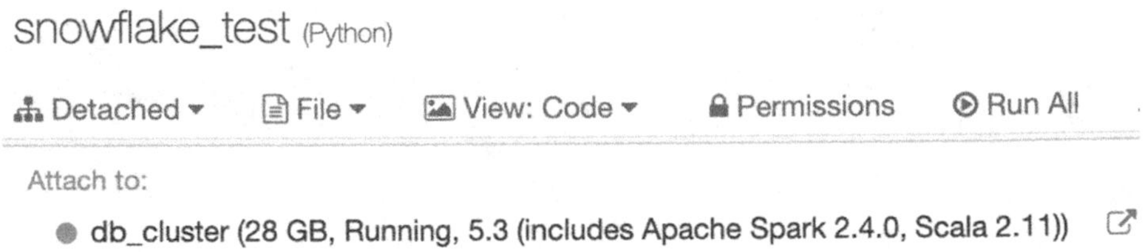

snowflake_test (Python)

⬡ Detached ▾   📄 File ▾   🖼 View: Code ▾   🔒 Permissions   ⦿ Run All

Attach to:

● db_cluster (28 GB, Running, 5.3 (includes Apache Spark 2.4.0, Scala 2.11))   ↗

Figure 12-8. *Attaching the cluster to a notebook*

---

[27]For more about optimizing performance with caching, see https://docs. databricks.com/delta/delta-cache.html.

7.   Connect to Snowflake.

Replace the substitutions according to your Snowflake credentials before executing Listing 12-1.

Caution   Best practice is to use Databricks *secrets*[28] instead of these substitutions. In Listing 12-1 we left substitutions for ease of perception.

Listing 12-1.   Connecting to Snowflake's TPCH_SF1.SNOWFLAKE_SAMPLE_DATA

```
options = dict(sfUrl="<your_snowflake_account>.
snowflakecomputing.com",
    sfUser="<user>",
    sfPassword="<password>",
    sfDatabase= "SNOWFLAKE_SAMPLE_DATA",
    sfSchema= "TPCH_SF1",
      sfWarehouse= "SMALL_COMPUTE_WH")
```

8.   Read data from Snowflake.

```
df = spark.read \
  .format("snowflake") \
  .options(**options) \
  .option("dbtable", "ORDERS") \
  .load()

display(df)
```

---

[28]For more about Databricks secrets, see https://docs.databricks.com/user-guide/secrets/index.html.

9.   Write data into Snowflake.

```
df.write \
    .format("snowflake") \
    .options(sfOptions) \
    .option("dbtable", "sampletable") \
    .mode(SaveMode.Overwrite) \
    .save() \
```

Summary

In this chapter, we covered how Snowflake works with modern analytics solutions. You learned about which popular advanced analytics platforms have deep integration with Snowflake and saw how this is done in practice by running through a quick example of Databricks.

In the next chapter, you will learn about how to migrate a legacy data warehouse system into Snowflake.

CHAPTER 13

Migrating to Snowflake

Throughout the book you have learned about key concepts of Snowflake, including its architecture and its security capabilities. You have also met some unique Snowflake features. Moreover, you saw how Snowflake can be integrated with third-party tools for ELT/ETL and BI purposes as well as big data and advanced analytics use cases with Spark.

In this chapter, we will highlight some key migration scenarios to give you an idea of how you can migrate your legacy solution to the cloud. In addition, some organizations might try to upgrade an existing cloud solution that isn't sufficient for a business use case or is very expensive.

Data warehouse modernization is the hottest topic right now, and many organizations are looking for best practices to modernize their legacy, expensive, and ineffective solutions using the cloud. Snowflake is a good choice for organizations because it is available on main cloud platforms such as Amazon Web Services (AWS), Microsoft Azure, and Google Cloud Platform (GCP), and it allows you to get instant value by democratizing the data across the organization.

In this chapter, we will cover the following topics:

- Data warehouse migration scenarios

- Common data architectures

© Dmitry Anoshin, Dmitry Shirokov, Donna Strok 2020
D. Anoshin et al., *Jumpstart Snowflake*, https://doi.org/10.1007/978-1-4842-5328-1_13

- Key steps for a data warehouse migration

- Real-world project

- Additional resources for Snowflake migration

Data Warehouse Migration Scenarios

The goal of a data warehouse migration is to serve the growing data appetite of end users who are hungry for data insights. Before we dive deep into this topic, let's categorize the organizations and their data needs. We will split organizations by their analytics maturity, as shown here:

- Startups and small business without a proper analytics solution

- Organizations with on-premise data solutions

- Organizations with a default cloud solution deployed on Azure, GCP, or AWS

Startup or Small Business Analytics Scenario

The easiest deployment process is for startup companies. They don't have any analytics solution yet and are usually connecting to source systems using business intelligence (BI) tool or spreadsheets. They are looking for better alternatives, and they don't want to invest in an expensive solution, but they want to be sure that they can start small and scale easily. With Snowflake, they get all the benefits of Snowflake and pay only for their workloads. Over time, they will grow, and as a result, their Snowflake implementation will grow.

Figure 13-1 shows an example architecture before Snowflake and with it for small companies.

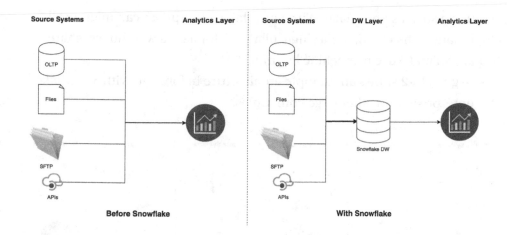

Figure 13-1. *Before and with Snowflake for startups*

Startups track key metrics, and it is important to get timely insights from data. As a result, analysts connect to the source systems and extract the data. This process is manual and not scalable. The next logical step is to hire a data engineer or analytics consulting company and deploy a data warehouse with Snowflake. This will allow you to get insights you're your data and grow the business.

On-Premise Analytics Scenario for Enterprises and Large Organizations

The second scenario is the biggest and the most popular. There are lots of enterprise organizations that are looking for a way to improve their existing on-premise solutions. These solutions are extremely expensive, and they require lots of resources to maintain. Moreover, they have lots of custom solutions for big data, streaming, and so on. The complexity of these solutions is extremely high, but the value isn't high because on-premise solutions are a bottleneck, and it is not easy to scale a solution even in the case of an unlimited budget. So, the best way is to migrate the existing on-premise solutions to the cloud and leverage an innovative analytics data platform such as Snowflake. With Snowflake, enterprises can migrate all their data to the cloud, use a single platform for a data warehouse, share data, and make use of machine learning.

Figure 13-2 shows an example architecture before and with Snowflake for enterprises and other large companies.

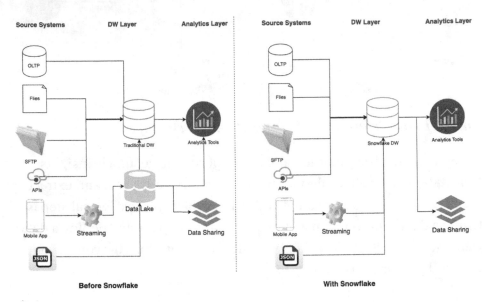

Figure 13-2. *Before and with Snowflake for enterprises*

The figure is a top-level overview of an on-premise organization with big data (a data lake, usually deployed on top of Hadoop) and an on-premise data warehouse massive parallel processing (MPP) solution such as Oracle, Teradata, or Netezza. Usually, enterprises use enterprise-grade ETL solutions that are expensive and require powerful hardware. There are multiple options for streaming, and one of the most popular is Apache Kafka. Moreover, enterprises handle a big volume of data with a semistructured format such as JSON, AVRO, Parquet, and so on. In the example in Figure 13-2, we are uploading JSON into a data lake and then parsing and loading it into a data warehouse. Finally, some organizations have to share data. This isn't an easy or cheap task for an on-premise solution.

With Snowflake, organizations will migrate all their data into the cloud. Moreover, they will use a single data platform for streaming use cases, storing semistructured data, and querying the data via SQL, without physically moving the data. So, there are lots of benefits that will open new horizons for analytics and help to make business decisions driven by data.

Cloud Analytics Modernization with Snowflake

The last scenario is the trickiest one. Some modern organizations have already leveraged cloud vendors or migrated a legacy solution to the cloud. However, they may be facing challenges such as high cost, performance issues related to concurrency, or having multiple tools for various business scenarios such as streaming and big data analytics. As a result, they decide to try Snowflake and unify their data analytics with a single platform and get almost unlimited scalability and elasticity.

Figure 13-3 shows an example architecture before and with Snowflake for cloud deployments with Microsoft Azure.

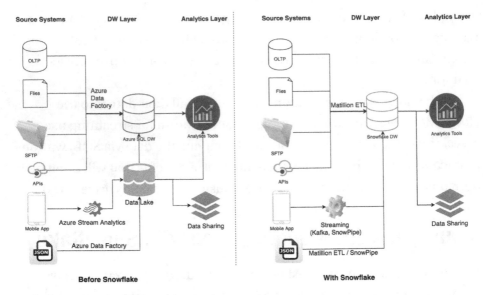

Figure 13-3. *Before and with Snowflake for cloud analytics modernization on Microsoft Azure*

On the left, we have multiple solutions from Azure for the data warehouse and data lake, such as Azure Data Factory and Azure Streaming. On the right, we have Snowflake that is hosted on the Azure cloud, and we have leveraged another cloud ELT tool, Matillion ETL, that allows us to create complex transformations visually. However, we can still use Azure Data Factory for ELT. Finally, with this new architecture, you can leverage the data sharing capabilities without physically moving the data.

Data Warehouse Migration Process

We just reviewed three common scenarios for Snowflake migrations. We will dive deep into the second scenario because it is one of the most popular and complex. The first scenario isn't a real migration scenario; it is more a DW design and implementation project. The third scenario is an evolution of the second; it has a similar idea, and usually it is easier to perform since all the data is already in the cloud.

When we talk about DW migration, there are two major approaches.

- **Lift and shift**: Just copy the data as is with limited changes.

- **Split and flip**: Split a solution into logical functional data layers. Match the data functionality with the right technology. Leverage the wide selection of tools on the cloud to best fit the needs. Move data in phases such as prototype, learn, and perfect.

Despite the fact that "lift and shift" is a faster approach, it has limited value for long-term organizational goals. As a result, we always prefer to "split and flip." This will guarantee that we won't sacrifice for short-term value.

We can split the migration process into two main buckets.

- The organizational part of the migration project

- The technical part of the migration project

Let's review them in detail.

Organizational Part of the Migration Project

Figure 13-4 shows a high-level overview of the steps needed to prepare and execute the migration of an existing system to Snowflake.

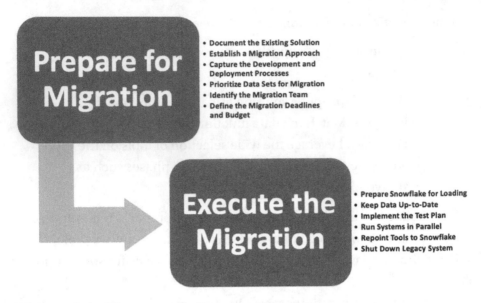

Prepare for Migration
- Document the Existing Solution
- Establish a Migration Approach
- Capture the Development and Deployment Processes
- Prioritize Data Sets for Migration
- Identify the Migration Team
- Define the Migration Deadlines and Budget

Execute the Migration
- Prepare Snowflake for Loading
- Keep Data Up-to-Date
- Implement the Test Plan
- Run Systems in Parallel
- Repoint Tools to Snowflake
- Shut Down Legacy System

Figure 13-4. *Key steps of migration process*

Let's learn more about each of migration steps that are recommended by Snowflake.

Document the Existing Solution

You already know that Snowflake uses row-based access control; therefore, we have to document the existing users, their roles, and their permissions. This allows you to replicate the data access and security strategy implemented in your legacy system. You should pay special attention to sensitive data sets and how they're secured, as well as how frequently security provisioning processes run in order to create similar security within Snowflake. Finally, you want to ensure that you have an existing architectural diagram of the existing solution.

Establish a Migration Approach

Then, you should establish a migration approach. You should list all the existing processes that you want to migrate. Moreover, you should identify all the processes that have to be refactored as well as the broken processes that need to be fixed. This will allow you to draft these deliverables and create the data architecture diagram to present to the stakeholders.

Snowflake generally recommends minimal re-engineering for the first iteration unless the current system is truly outdated. To provide a value for the business as soon as possible, you should avoid a single "big-bang" deliverable as the migration approach and instead break the migration into incremental deliverables that enable your organization to start making the transition to Snowflake more quickly. This process is called *agile data warehousing* and allows you to deliver fast value for the end users.

Moreover, organizations may want to change their development or deployment processes as part of the migration. You should document new tools that will be introduced as a result of the migration, tools that will need to be deprecated, and development environments that are needed for the migration. Whether the development and deployment processes change or not, you should capture the development environments that will be used for the migration.

Capture the Development and Deployment Processes

Modern organizations care about DevOps. If you didn't widely use it before, it could be a good opportunity to start implementing DevOps/DataOps procedures that will increase the quality of your analytics solution.

For example, usually organizations have the following environments:

- Dev

- QA

- Prod

Moreover, they have source control repositories and methods for capturing deployment changes from one environment to another. These will be used for that migration. This information is critical to direct how the development and deployments are implemented.

The ideal candidates for starting the migration provide value to the business and require a minimal migration effort.

Prioritize Data Sets for Migration

You should learn more about the available data sets in the legacy solutions. Rather than starting with the most complex data sets, we prefer to begin with a simple data set that can be migrated quickly to establish a foundation through the development and deployment processes that can be reused for the rest of the migration effort. To prioritize data sets for migration, you should understand the dependencies among data sets. Those dependencies need to be documented and conform with business stakeholders. Ideally, this documentation can be captured using an automated process that collects information from existing ETL jobs, job schedules, and so on. This will help you avoid manual work for identifying and documenting changes.

Creating an automated process provides value throughout the migration project by more easily identifying the ongoing changes that will occur throughout the migration project since the underlying systems are unlikely to be static during the migration.

Identify the Migration Team

Another important thing is to build the migration team. Some common roles needed for the migration are developer, quality assurance, business owner, project manager, program manager, scrum master, and communication. When a Snowflake solution partner is engaged for migration, they may fulfill multiple needs, including solution design, gathering requirements, delivering migration project, producing documentation and conducting Snowflake training.

Based on our experience, the challenge is to change the paradigm from a traditional DW to a cloud DW. Engineers should be ready to learn new skills, and they may apply for additional professional courses related to cloud foundations and Snowflake best practices.

Define the Migration Deadlines and Budget

The expectations for any migration should be clear to all parties. But the expectations need to be combined with other information that has been gathered to determine whether the deadlines can be met. One of the benefits of gathering all of this information is to establish and communicate achievable deadlines, even if the deadlines are different from what the business expects.

It is common in migration projects that deadlines are defined before evaluating the scope of the project to determine whether the deadlines are achievable, especially if the business is trying to deprecate the legacy system before the renewal date. In situations where the deadline can't be moved and the migration scope requires more time than is available before the deadline, work needs to be done with the business to agree on a path forward.

Understanding the budget that has been advocated to complete the migration is also critically important. The amount of migration work and the cost associated with the migration work both need to be compared to the available budget to ensure that there are sufficient funds to complete the work. Pausing in the middle of a migration or stopping it altogether is a bad outcome for all involved parties.

When we are planning the budget, we should estimate the cost of Snowflake deployment and the cost of the migration project.

Determine the Migration Outcomes

Migration outcomes should be used to validate that the migration project is providing the overall benefit the business expects to achieve from the migration. For example, turning off the Oracle database system is one of the desired outcomes. That outcome should be achieved with the migration plan. This documentation can be expressed as success or failure criteria for the migration project and may also include benchmarks that compare process execution. Once compiled, this information should be used for communicating with stakeholders.

After identifying the migration outcomes, you should present them to the business along with the mitigation strategy and confirm the proposed approach will meet their requirements. This should be done to set appropriate expectations from the beginning of the migration.

The escalation process needs to be documented, including who is responsible for working on the issue, who is responsible for communicating the progress of the issue, and a list of contexts from the business, Snowflake, and any other involved parties that are involved in resolving the issue.

Establish Security

Depending on the security requirements, there may be a need to capture role creation, user creation, and the granting of users to roles for auditing purposes. While the existing database security can be a good starting point for setting up security within Snowflake, the security model should be evaluated to determine whether there are roles and users who are no longer needed or should be implemented differently as part of the migration to Snowflake. Additional roles may be required for restricting access to sensitive data. Moreover, you can think about improving the solution security by implementing two-step authentication, collecting security logs, and so on.

Develop a Test Plan

Develop a test plan by identifying the appropriate level and scope for each environment. For example, schedules aren't executed in dev, but only in QA and prod. Automate as much possible to ensure repeatable test processes with consistent output for validation purposes and to find agreed-on document acceptance criteria.

Moreover, you should involve business users in this process; they are subject-matter experts and will help to evaluate solutions and help you quickly identify the data discrepancy and processes that are wrong.

Prepare Snowflake for Loading

Despite that Snowflake is a SQL data warehouse, it is different from other analytical DW platforms.

When you have physical servers, you can use a dedicated server for each environment (dev, test, prod). The hierarchy for the on-premise solution looks like this:

- Physical server

- Databases

    - Schemas

        - Tables/views/functions

In the case of Snowflake, you don't have a physical machine. When you sign up for Snowflake, you get the link `https://<our company name>.snowflakecomputing.com/`, and you stick to this account. As a result, you don't have a physical server layer, and you should think about the organization of environments. To solve this particular issue, you have several options.

- Use multiple accounts (different URLs).

- Create many databases with an environment prefix (FIN_DEV, SALES_DEV, FIND_TEST, and so on).

- Create databases that will represent your environments and then create a schema that will represent a database.

This will require you to modify DDL while you are moving the schema from the on-premise solution to the cloud. This is one of the biggest engineering efforts in a migration. There are a number of tools available for this purpose that can do forward and reverse engineering. Moreover, you can leverage the Snowflake community and learn how others performed this step.

Finally, you should assign databases, database objects, and virtual warehouses to the appropriate security roles.

When you are ready, you can start to make an initial load into your data warehouse. Many options are available for loading. For example, you can unload data into the cloud storage, such as S3 in the case of using AWS, and then collect this data via Snowflake. Or you can leverage cloud ETL tools like Glue (AWS product) or Matillion ETL (a third-party commercial product). You can even use open source solutions like Apache Airflow or even Python.

Keep Data Up-to-Date (Executing the Migration)

After an initial load of data is complete, you should start to develop incremental load processes. This is the time when ETL/ELT tools are handy and help you to accelerate your development effort.

These processes should be scheduled and take into consideration the appropriate process dependency. The state of the data loading should be clearly understood and communicated. For example, loading is in progress, loading is completed successfully, and load failures occurred that need to be addressed. Finally, begin comparing execution timings to ensure that SLAs are being met.

One of the key things is to constantly communicate with business users and allow them to visually track the load process. You can ensure this by collecting ETL logs on all stages of the ETL process and visualize it with BI tool.

Implement the Test Plan (Executing the Migration)

Once an ETL/ELT process is in place, testing can begin. You can start from initial data comparisons. This will allow for quickly identifying discrepancies and sharing these results with stakeholders. Additional groups should be engaged after the initial testing is completed. This helps to validate the data and fix issues within a new solution.

Run Systems in Parallel (Executing the Migration)

As business units are engaged in testing, you should run both systems (legacy DW and Snowflake DW) in parallel to ensure the continued validation of data to facilitate comparing data. In some cases, you may export data from a legacy DW, which can be used for comparing data at the raw level. These comparisons should take place in Snowflake, where resources can be provisioned to compare data without negatively impacting the system.

You should attempt to minimize the time the two systems are running in parallel while still maintaining a sufficient validation process.

Repoint Tools to Snowflake

Up until now, the migration process has been focused on raw data comparisons. The final step is to point all business users' connections to the new Snowflake DW. After the business units have validated that their tools are producing required results, they cut over to Snowflake, begin scheduling, and communicate the cutover plans to all stakeholders.

Once the cutover is complete, users should have the ability to log into Business Intelligence tools and repoint them to the Snowflake data warehouse.

Technical Aspects of a Migration Project

Figure 13-5 shows the key elements of a migration project from a technical point of view for a traditional on-premise data warehouse.

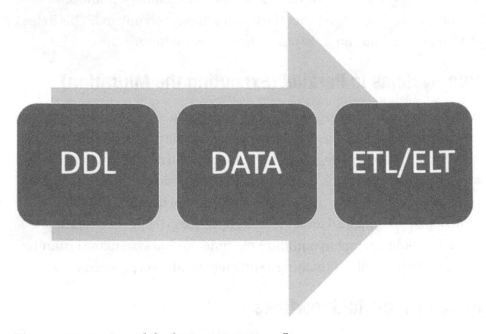

Figure 13-5. *Simplified DW migration flow*

Let's consider an example where we have an on-premise DW that we have decided to move to Snowflake. We should start with the DDL for moving the schemas, tables, views, and so on. There are many ways to replicate a data warehouse model in Snowflake, starting from the Python scripts that will convert the source system's DDL into Snowflake DDL. In addition, we can leverage data modeling tools like SQLDbm that have good integration with Snowflake and can copy the source system DDL, convert it to Snowflake DDL, and deploy it into Snowflake. Moreover, we can use other tools that support forward and reverse engineering. This will help us automate this process and save time and money.

After the DDL, we should move data. There are many approaches to do this. We can leverage cloud ETL tool capabilities and migrate data from an on-premise solution to Snowflake. For example, Matillion ETL can connect to the on-premise DW and load data directly to Snowflake using cloud data storage such as S3, Blob Storage, and so on. This is an efficient way of moving data. Or, you could leverage Snowflake's snowSQL CLI and load data with the help of SQL. It is totally up to you. In some extreme cases for a large volume of data, we might use physical devices such as AWS Snowball or Azure Data Box.

Finally, the most complicated part is migrating the ETL/ELT logic. This is the longest part, and there is a linear correlation between the number of DW objects and the time it takes to perform a migration. This is the time when we want to decide whether we want to migrate existing logic as is (lift and shift) or we want to work closely with the business stakeholders and learn about the business logic behind the code so we can take it apart and improve it (split and flip).

From a tools standpoint, we can leverage scripting in Python, or we can leverage Snowflake Partner Connect and choose an ETL tool that was built specifically for the Snowflake DW. Some tools are managed services, and others give you more freedom. For example, Matillion provides a virtual machine that is hosted in our virtual private cloud (VPC), and we can establish a mature security level. Moreover, when we are using ETL tools, we can create a pattern, and then we can copy this pattern across the use cases. The tools also allow end users to follow the process and visually observe the data flow. Finally, Snowflake supports stored procedures, and this gives you the ability to implement an ETL solution with stored procedures like previously done in Oracle, Teradata, or SQL Server.

Real-World Migration Project

Let's look at a real-world project. Figure 13-6 shows an architecture diagram for an e-commerce company that is selling used books online.

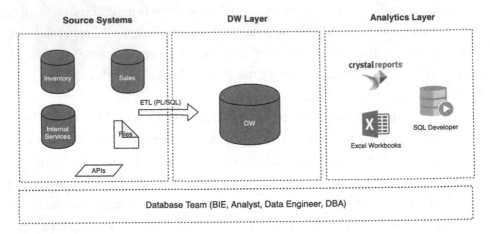

Figure 13-6. *Legacy DW architecture*

It is a straightforward solution that was built on an Oracle database technology stack. It used PL/SQL as a main ETL tool, and with daily ETL, it was loading data from several transactional systems as well as consuming data from marketing-specific APIs and SFTPs. These were the challenges:

- The solution was expensive from a license perspective.

- ETL was complicated, and the database team owned the logic. They were a kind of bottleneck for all new requests.

- The DW had storage and compute limitations.

- The DW required full-time DBA support (for patching, backups, and so on).

- Performance was an issue and required deep knowledge of Oracle sizing and tuning (indexes, keys, partitions, query plans, and so on).

The company decided to move to the cloud to get more room to grow and to get the benefits of a cloud infrastructure. Figure 13-7 shows an architecture diagram of the new solution. This organization decided to go with Snowflake, because it wanted to have unlimited concurrency for queries, a consolidated DW, and a big data solution on a single data platform, as well as dedicated virtual warehouses for analysts with heavy queries.

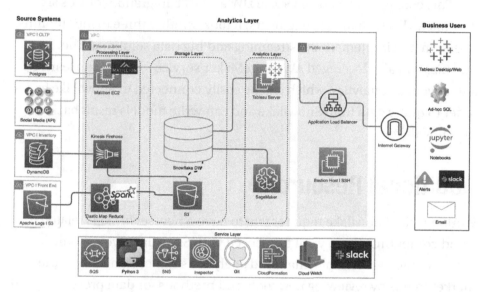

Figure 13-7. *Modern DW architecture with Snowflake*

Another major decision was made regarding the ETL tool. We reviewed several tools and decided to go with Matillion ETL, because it was built specifically for Snowflake and allows us to solve previous challenges with "bottlenecks" in the ETL process. It has an intuitive user interface and doesn't require any coding knowledge. In addition, the organization deployed Tableau as a main BI tool and settled on self-service analytics; that's why concurrency is a great benefit of Snowflake. Moreover, the choice addressed another security requirement because it deploys within a private subnet in AWS VPC.

247

Snowflake helped us to leverage big data and streaming capabilities that were impossible with the legacy solution. For big data, we were processing web logs within Apache Spark deployed on top of the EMR cluster. Snowflake accesses Parquet files, and we don't need to load them into Snowflake. For the streaming use case, we leveraged DynamoDB streams and Kinesis Firehose, and all data is sent into an S3 bucket where Snowflake can consume it.

This core project with an Oracle DW and ETL migration took us six months with a team of two engineers; it took another three to four months to design and implement the streaming and big data solutions. The organization also leveraged AWS SageMaker service for machine learning and advanced analytics, which can be easily connected to Snowflake in order to query data from Snowflake and can write models result back to the Snowflake.

Additional Resources

Working with Snowflake requires you to have a new set of skills related to cloud computing. If you want to succeed with Snowflake, you should learn the best practices of deploying cloud analytics solutions and follow the market trends by reviewing new tools and methods for data processing and transformation in the cloud.

Currently Snowflake is available in AWS, Microsoft Azure, and Google Cloud Platform. We highly recommend you study a cloud vendor's learning materials in order to get a better understanding of cloud computing and data storage. For example, if you deploy Snowflake using AWS, you may start with the AWS Technical Essentials course that is free and gives you an overview of AWS. Then you can go deeper with AWS analytics using big data specialization.

At the same time, you should learn Snowflake best practices using Snowflake training resources, community web sites, and blog posts. This book is a good start.

Summary

This chapter talked about the needs of organizations depending on their maturity model and identified three common organization types. Then you learned about the legacy DW modernization process and identified the key steps.

Finally, we looked at a real-world project of migrating to Snowflake and learned about its data architecture and project outcome.

CHAPTER 14

Time Travel

This chapter will cover the following tasks:

- Working with previous versions of objects. In other words, Snowflake provides the ability to query historical data.

- Creating copies/backups of data on the technical history of objects.

A specialty of the technical design of the Snowflake is that the data is stored in micro-partitions,[1] which are immutable. This means that with any operations such as the addition or deletion of data, a new micro-partition is created, and the old one ceases to exist. Using special commands that extend standard SQL, you can easily access historical data.

In general, the user's data in a system has the following lifecycle:

- Data is created in data storage.

- Depending on the license, all states of the data are stored during the *retention period* (Table 14-1). Users can work with a technical history of any object using SQL extensions.

---

[1] https://docs.snowflake.net/manuals/user-guide/tables-clustering-micropartitions.html

© Dmitry Anoshin, Dmitry Shirokov, Donna Strok 2020
D. Anoshin et al., *Jumpstart Snowflake*, https://doi.org/10.1007/978-1-4842-5328-1_14

- At the end of the term, data moves to a particular zone called *fail-safe*.[2] Accordingly, the actual data of the object, together with the related technical history, becomes inaccessible to the user. In this area, data is stored for seven days and can be recoverable only by Snowflake.

Table 14-1. *Data Retention Period Depending on License*

License	Description
Standard Edition	The default is one day. (This can be set to zero days.)
Snowflake Enterprise Edition and higher	For permanent objects, the range is from 0 to 90 days. For transient[3] objects, the default is one day. The range is from zero to one day.

The parameter DATA_RETENTION_TIME_IN_DAYS can be set on the whole account or on the object level, meaning database, schema, or table. According to this hierarchy, the parameter can be overridden.

The Snowflake Time Travel SQL extension provides some groups of statements:

- Querying any version of data of the table using the following:

  - The statement *SELECT* with *AT/BEFORE*

  - The user can request the version of the table by specifying the exact time (using keyword *TIMESTAMP*)

---

[2]https://docs.snowflake.net/manuals/user-guide/data-failsafe.html
[3]https://docs.snowflake.net/manuals/user-guide/tables-temp-transient.html

For example, to get data on August 5, 2019, use this:

```
SELECT * FROM <table> AT (TIMESTAMP => 'Mon,
05 Aug 2019 13:30:00 -0700'::timestamp);
```

- The user can request the version of the table by specifying the relative time, meaning the time difference in seconds from the present time (using keyword *OFFSET*).

  For example, select historical data from a table of 30 minutes ago using this:

  ```
  SELECT * FROM <table> AT (offset -60*30)
  ```

- *STATEMENT* identifier of a certain transaction. Here's an example:

  ```
  SELECT * FROM <table> BEFORE (STATEMENT =>
  '<statement_id>');
  ```

- Creating a clone of a table, a schema, or a whole database using the *CREATE <TABLE>|<SCHEMA>| <DB> CLONE . <ORIG_OBJECT>* statement

  Here's an example:

  ```
  CREATE TABLE <table_restored> CLONE <original_table>);
  ```

- Restoring an object using the *UNDROP <TABLE>|<SCHEMA>|<DB>* command. Here's an example:

  ```
  UNDROP TABLE <table>
  ```

- Additionally, the command SHOW TABLE HISTORY helps track versions of an object.

Figure 14-1 shows an example. Table 14-2 describes the process.

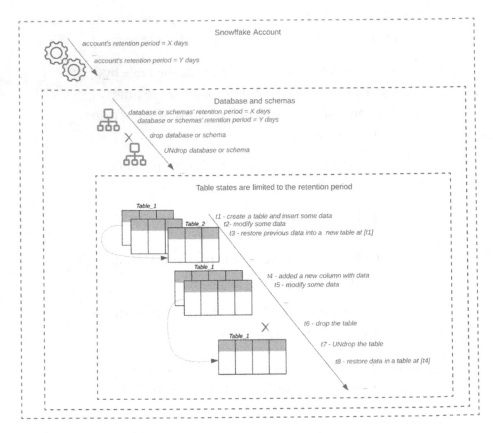

Figure 14-1. *Time Travel feature in Snowflake*

Table 14-2. *Working with Time Travel*

Steps	Description
1	The user sets the retention period for the account to X and then to Y using the ALTER .. SET statement. Accordingly, this strategy applies to all objects in the account.
2	The user sets the retention period for the database or schema to X and then Y using the ALTER .. SET statement. This means that the retention time will be changed for all objects below the hierarchy.
3	The user DROPs the database or schema and then UNDROPs it without any problems because the retention time has not expired yet.
4	The user creates a new table called Table_1 and then adds some data. This means at a point in time, t1, the table contains certain data. Further, the user updates some rows in the table, so, at the time point t2, the table already has other data.
5	The user creates a new table called Table_2 with the previous state of table Table_1 at point of time t1 using the statement SELECT with AT t1 or SELECT with *t1*.
6	This mechanism also supports schema evolution, which means the user can add a new column to the table and add values into a new column. The user can request any version of the table, and data will be returned in the format it was in at the time of the request.
7	The last step is that the user can DROP and UNDROP the table and also can CREATE a new table as CLONE at any point in time during the retention time.

TIME TRAVEL FEATURE

Let's look at how to use the Time Travel feature in practice.

1. Log into your Snowflake account.

2. Switch to Worksheets and execute the code in Listing 14-1 to check the current data retention parameter.

Listing 14-1. Checking Retention Parameters and Trying to Change Them

```
show parameters like '%DATA_RETENTION%' in account;
alter account set DATA_RETENTION_TIME_IN_DAYS = 2;

show parameters like '%DATA%_RETENTION' in database samples;
alter database samples
  set DATA_RETENTION_TIME_IN_DAYS = 1;
```

In Listing 14-1, we did the following:

- We checked the current data retention parameter for the account using the `show parameters..` in account command.

- We changed the parameter to two days for the account using the `alter account..set` command.

- We checked the current data retention parameter for the database using the `show parameters..in account` command. We can see that it changed to 2. Since all objects are attached to an account, the account parameters are automatically applied to all objects below the hierarchy.

- We changed the parameter to 1 for the database using the `alter database..set` command. See Figure 14-2.

Row	key	value	default	level	description	type
1	DATA_RETENTION_TIME_IN_DAYS	1	1		number of days to retain the old version of deleted/updated data	NUMBER

Figure 14-2. *Data retention parameter*

3. Create a new sample table for the example by executing the code in Listing 14-2.

Listing 14-2. Creating a New Table

```
create or replace table samples.finance.stocks (
   id int,
    symbol string,
    name string);

insert into samples.finance.stocks
       values(1,'TDC', 'Teradata'),
       (2,'ORCL', 'Oracle'),
       (3,'TSLA', 'Tesla');

select * from samples.finance.stocks;
```

In Listing 14-2, we did the following:

- We created a new empty table called stocks.

- We populated the table with values. See Figure 14-3.

Row	ID	SYMBOL	NAME
1	1	TDC	Teradata
2	2	ORCL	Oracle
3	3	TSLA	Tesla

Figure 14-3. *Sample table*

4. Modify the table and try to query the previous state. Wait about a minute after the previous commands and execute the code in Listing 14-3.

257

Listing 14-3. Changing Data in the Table and Checking the State of the Table

```
insert into samples.finance.stocks
values(5,'MSFT', 'Microsoft');
  delete from samples.finance.stocks
  where id = 3;
select * from samples.finance.stocks;
select * from samples.finance.stocks at
(offset => -1*60);
```

In Listing 14-3, we did the following:

- We changed the data in the table, inserted a new row, and deleted one row.

- We checked the current state of the table. See Figure 14-4.

Row	ID	SYMBOL	NAME
1	1	TDC	Teradata
2	2	ORCL	Oracle
3	5	MSFT	Microsoft

Figure 14-4. *The last state of the table*

- We checked the state minutes ago using the following. See Figure 14-5.

  at (offset => -1*60).

Row	ID	SYMBOL	NAME
1	1	TDC	Teradata
2	2	ORCL	Oracle
3	3	TSLA	Tesla

Figure 14-5. *The previous state of the table*

5.   Drop and undrop the table, as shown in Listing 14-4.

Listing 14-4. Changing the Data in the Table and Checking the State of the Table

```
drop table samples.finance.stocks;
select * from samples.finance.stocks;
   undrop table samples.finance.stocks;
```

6.   Create a new table as a clone of the previous state of the original table. Execute the code in Listing 14-5.

Listing 14-5. Creating a Clone of the Table

```
create table samples.finance.stocks_10m clone
   samples.finance.stocks at (offset => -10*60);
```

Summary

In this chapter, we covered the Time Travel feature. Moreover, you learned about the data lifecycle in Snowflake and how to work with the history of data objects in Snowflake.

Finally, we walked you through a few examples using the Time Travel feature.

Index

A

Administration
    clustered tables, 124, 125
    database objects, 122, 123
    databases, 118, 119
    data share, 123, 124
    parameters, 121, 122
    warehouses, 117, 118
Advanced Encryption Standard
    (AES), 136
Agile data warehousing, 237
ALTER WAREHOUSE
    command, 118
Alteryx, 214
Amazon Web Services (AWS), 20, 229
Analytical ecosystem, 214
Apache MLflow, 215
Apache Spark, 214, 222
    cloud providers, 216
    components, 216, 217
    connector
        data flow process, 218
        key features, 219
        stages, 218
    data scientists, 216
    machine learning, 215
    optimal strategy, 216
    vs. Snowflake, 219, 220

AVRO file
    generation, 169
    JSON sample file, 168
    loading data, 171
    metadata, 169
    schema, 168
    working, 167
AWS Snowball, 245
Azure Data Box, 245
Azure Databricks, 222
    connecting Snowflake, 227
    creation, 223, 224
    data, 227, 228
    delta caching, 226
    environment, 224, 225
    notebook, 226
    Spark cluster, 225, 226

B

Batch method, 197
Bulk data loading
    compression methods, 57
    COPY statement, 54
    encoding, 56
    encryption, 57
    file formats, 55, 56
    staging area, 54

Printed in the United States
By Bookmasters